My Story

Miracles Happen **Every Day**

Faith + Courage + Cancer

Jacque Massaglia

CreateSpace Publishing
CreateSpace

Hays, KS 67601

All rights reserved. No part of this book may be used or reproduced in any manner without written permission from the author(s) and publisher.

This work is solely for personal growth and education. It should not be treated as a substitute for professional assistance, therapeutic activities such as psychotherapy or counseling, or medical advice of any type.

Published 2017

Cover design by Patrick Harris, PH Creative, www.patrickharriscreative.com

Cover image by Dreamstime

Book Design by Patrick Harris, PH Creative, www.patrickharriscreative.com

Printed in the United States of America

Library of Congress Cataloging-in Publication Data

Massaglia, Jacque, 1957-

My Story... Miracles Happen Every Day – Faith, Courage and Cancer / J. Massaglia. p.cm.

ISBN 978-0997017915

EBook 978-00997017915

CONTENTS

		Page
	Acknowledgments	
	Prologue	
1	A Brief History (I Hope)	1
2	The Beginning...	7
3	The Hard Facts about Pancreatic Cancer	13
4	Matt's First E-mail to the Family	19
5	Digression Number One	23
6	Radiation...	25
7	Spiffy Inspiration from Matt	27
8	FINE is the Answer	31
9	Chemo...	35
10	Thankful Update	39
11	The Story Continues	41
12	Free at Last	45
13	Ongoing Battle	49
14	All Earthly Powers Exhausted	53
15	Clock is Unknown	55

16	Funeral Planning	59
17	The Wow Factor	61
18	Spreading the Good News	65
19	The Tumor is Dead	67
20	Living with the Good News	71
21	And the Saga Continues	75
22	Praise the Lord – Best Case Scenario	77
23	Dare to be UN-PC (Politically Correct)	79
24	Pets and Cats	81
25	The Sermon	83
26	The Quiet Years	91
27	The Good, the Bad and the Beautiful	93
28	Goodbye 2013, Welcome 2014 (Maybe)	97
29	This is not the End	101

ACKNOWLEDGMENTS

I have so many things to be thankful for. First and foremost I thank my Heavenly Father for giving me more time on this earth to be with family and friends. This illness has taught me many things, but most of all how Jesus is in my life daily holding my hand through the good and tough times.

It goes without saying that my husband Matt has been my earthly rock. In one of his e-mails he wrote all the things I am to him and I can say he is just as much if not more to me. He continues to be my caregiver. When asked by the Wesley staff if he would get queasy changing my bandage, I had to contain my laughter. Dr. Gronlie has been the main doctor I have had for my bilinary tube changes, but others have done the procedure too. They always comment on how well he keeps my wound clean and ask me what he does for a living. My response is, "He is a maintenance engineer; you know plumbing a building or plumbing your wife pretty much the same thing." Needless to say I usually get a chuckle or two!

I don't know how to begin to thank my lovely cousin Val. I may not excel at English, but she sure does. She is my editor. She has put the polish on this book and kept me from violating any writers' laws. Without her this would just be words on paper with nowhere to go.

This cannot end without thanking all my family,

through blood or friendship, for all their support before, during and after my cancer. Mom has been a rock, sometimes a little too motherly, but I know it is because of her love for me. Sometimes I am mothered by others too. I admit it gets a little frustrating at times, but I know they care and I love them for that love.

Finally, I would like to thank you for reading this book. Is does a writer no good to put into words the hard fought battle if no one chooses to read the book. **My wish is that whatever struggles you may face in life, you remember that the battles can be won.** May God bless each and every one of you.

PROLOGUE

"Have mercy on me, Oh God, according to thy steadfast Love; according to thy abundant mercy blot out my transgressions."RSV Bible Psalms 51:1

"My Story... Miracles Happen Every Day" is written for all of those who prayed for me during my illness and have since said, "Why don't you write a book?" My big hesitation on putting it into words was I am not a writer and did not even care for English that much in school. Also time was a factor, but since I had lost my job and the job search was slow I thought why not give it a try. *My goal in writing this is to encourage others who face dire circumstances and to give them hope.*

This story tells about my journey with stage IV pancreatic cancer, and also includes the caregiver's viewpoint from my husband Matt.

Pancreatic cancer is known as the silent killer...

You Are Here...

It might be helpful to some of you to understand the location of where this story happened.

Hays, Kansas, our place of residence, is located halfway between Kansas City and Denver on Interstate 70. Hays Medical Center is here and I was able to do all my chemo and radiation in my hometown. The oncology staff here is top notch and became part of our extended family after taking care of both Matt and me during our treatments. Coming from a city of a population of about 25,000, it is easy to run into people around town; it truly is a city where everyone knows your name.

Salina, Kansas is 90 miles east on Interstate 70. We had my scopes done at Salina Regional Medical Center by Dr. Johnson from the Mowery Clinic. Dr. Johnson's hospital team was some of our biggest cheerleaders.

Denver, Colorado is about five and a half hours west on Interstate 70 and this is where we stayed with my Aunt Darlene and Uncle Ron and also saw the specialist in the field, Dr. Kortz.

Kansas City, Missouri is where we went to see Dr. Jafri, a little over five hours east on Interstate 70. As the RN inserted my IV needle, she said, "Welcome to our "bed and breakfast." Just my kind of humor...

Wichita, Kansas is where Wesley Medical Center is located and is where we travel every time I need my bilinary tube replaced. It is 90 miles east on Interstate 70 to Salina and then 90 miles from Salina to Wichita on Interstate 135. We have gotten to know this staff very well, almost to the point I think we need to exchange Christmas cards. What a great team!

I would like to thank the staff and doctors at each and every one of these institutions. What amazing people this journey has brought into our lives. If any of you chance to read this, know that we felt God put each one of you into our lives just at the right time; He knew we needed you, making you all part of this miracle too.

1 - A BRIEF HISTORY (I HOPE)

"When you are courting a nice girl an hour seems like a second. When you sit on a red-hot cinder a second seems like an hour. That's relativity."
– Albert Einstein

Matt & I met working in a restaurant when we were fifteen and sixteen. And as they say, from there it was history. We married when Matt graduated from high school, and almost 40 years later, we are still in love. We had our first child, a boy we named Steven, almost two years later. As most new parents, we questioned our ability to raise a child. I thought I would be a stay-at-home mom, but Steven was such a good baby I found myself bored. So I went to work at a local manufacturing firm. The problem was I had to work second shift for ten months and Matt worked days at his job, so we basically only saw each other on weekends. This was probably the biggest hurdle of our married life. A little over three years later, we had our second child, a girl we named Brina. I was working day shift by then, but almost my whole check was going to day care, so I went to third shift.

Life went on. We had ups and downs in our jobs, layoffs, closures, things we over which we had no control. Finally things settled down. Our children married; contrary to popular belief we kind of liked the empty nest. Don't get me wrong, we love our children and love when they visit, but we also love being together alone.

Our son had been married for a few years and the usual question for parents to ask is, "When do we get some grandchildren?" And a little guilt, "You know we had you when we were young so that you would have lots of time with your grandparents." That is something Matt and I never had, being the youngest in our families. Our son's reply was, "You guys are still young, and we have plenty of time." I never asked, but I often wondered if he ever thought about saying that to us. Brina got married in 2005 and at that time Steven and Danielle were expecting their first child; Erin was born in December.

Life was good. The Lord has blessed us in so many ways over the years. We had good children, not perfect but good. Neither one was into drugs or drinking. They made good choices in the friends they made. It was hard getting them to do chores around the house, but surprise of all, they both learned how to keep a household, the responsibility of paying bills and holding down a job. They also made good choices in the spouses they married, know marriage is work and that you don't give up with the first bump. We may not boast the biggest banks accounts, but we have everything we need and a lot of our wants too.

Then May 2006 arrived. Matt woke up on a Saturday morning and said, "I think I need to go to the ER." Those are words that were never said before, but have been said too much since then. We went in thinking it was his appendix and we were right, only it was much more than that. It was his appendix, but with a twist. An appendix should be the size of your little finger; his was the size of a flip phone. It was a tumor. It was cancer. It was scary. A week later he would have his second surgery to remove about eight inches of his colon. I said before I did not care for English class; well I did not think much of biology either. Since then I have learn firsthand more than I ever thought I would want to know. We started the long journey of chemo treatments for Matt. He first had to recover from the surgeries before he could begin treatments. During his second surgery they had installed a port, so once he recovered he could start the process. He had treatments every other week, and went home with a pump over the weekend.

That was until his port blew out his of skin on, of all nights, Halloween. So off to ER we went again. A fun sidebar to this night is that I was taken from the ER room and Matt's side to answer questions for a police officer. It seems someone coming to the hospital had blown passed some other car on the way and had jumped out of their vehicle and run into the ER doors and disappeared. So the police were questioning everyone who was in the ER. To make a long story short, I did not drive the vehicle in question. But that is how our life goes. You have to see the humor! If you can't make lemonade out of lemons, then you need to learn.

With the loss of the port he was now going to receive treatments in his arm every third week and take a series of pills. The craziness of this is that even though he went home with the pump on weekends and the insurance covered this, now that he was going to be on pills, it did not provide coverage. To me drugs are drugs. I am not complaining about our insurance company; they have been great, but I just question the system itself. Thanks to our excellent oncology nurse, she worked with our insurance and a mail-order pharmaceutical company and got the cost of the chemo pills to a price we could afford. It was also a blessing that we had cancer insurance. We would have had to declare bankruptcy if not for that.

I remember one evening when we were watching TV and talking and I told him I get to die first (this had been said a number of times before, just because I couldn't imagine life without Matt). He looked at me and said, "We know that isn't going to happen." This was an evening early in his treatments and we were still coming to grips with the cancer. I said in response, "Well you know how many times other drivers like to run into me." And it was true. Even though I avoided a lot of close calls, other drivers still hit me. Matt and I joke about it now, but we swear we are invisible when we get behind a wheel of a car. Also on another such evening Matt said, "Don't you ever get sick, because I will not be able to take as good of care of you as you have been taking of me." Both these conversations would come back to haunt us.

I think now is a good time to add in a note of my selfishness. When we first got the news of Matt's cancer and he was still in the hospital I had too much time reflect. I was out on the patio one night and my first thought was I am too young to be a widow. Matt was only 48 and I was 49. I couldn't imagine life without him. You have to remember that in those years a lot of people were still dying of colon cancer. That is what they were treating his as since they had removed his appendix. I guess I add this just to let you know I am human.

Life went on. I believe Matt finished his treatments in December or January. They had to be postponed a few times because his white blood cell count got too low. We got into a schedule, between doctors' appointments, blood work, our jobs and family as we settled into our new routine. A little note here is if you have ever had or someone close to you have cancer, there becomes a new normal in your life. It can be compared to but is still very different from normal life with changes such as marriage, children, jobs and so forth. It is hard to explain but a good example of this is getting blood work done. If you have had blood work done you have seen the parameters for good numbers. Well after having treatments those parameters go out the window. All you hope for is for them to go up or down in the right direction.

By this point you a probably wondering what "My Story" is. I am coming to that, but felt a little background would help you understand it and us a little better...

2 – THE BEGINNING...

"In the end, it's not the years in your life that count. It's the life in your years." – Abraham Lincoln

On Valentine's Day in 2008 we went out to dinner with Brina and Lance. The next couple of days I did not feel real well, and thought maybe it was the flu or food poisoning. I continued to go to work each day and I felt a little better. I might note at this point I was a production manager for an athletic-wear company, Stromgrens. In that position I handled a major buyer's order in packaging them per store and everything involved with that. It was either the first or second week of March that I started losing weight. I lost ten pounds in one week and although I thought this is great (I was overweight at the time), I knew something was wrong. After I finished one of the work orders mentioned above, I went to my boss and said I think I am going to call Matt to take me to the ER. *The only way I can describe my symptoms is that it felt like life was leaving my body.*

After arriving at the ER we did the normal sitting in the waiting room routine. As with everywhere now, they have TVs in the waiting room. *The news that day was Patrick Swayze had just announced that he had pancreatic cancer* and Brett Favre was crying that he was retiring, to which Matt said, "Man up, Brett."

Finally we were lead to a room. I apologized to all the ER doctors we have seen over the last eight years, there have been too many, rarely did we see the same one twice and sometimes I can't remember their names. Not to mention that with the stress of going to the ER, names are the last things on your mind.

The ER doctor came in and asked a few questions. This doctor (I really wish I could remember his name) was pretty straightforward with us and strongly hinted at pancreatic cancer, and actually another doctor there frowned at him for doing so. I am one of those people who do not like to be treated with kid gloves. Even though I don't have a lot of medical knowledge or mechanical knowledge of cars and such, don't talk to me like I can't or won't ever understand. I might note at this time that I went to the ER because I was unable to get into my regular doctor or any other doctors in town. Not to discount any of them, I believe God lead me this way because of the urgency. Going through regular channels would have slowed down the process even more. I think they did a scan and probably a bunch of other tests, but I don't remember everything as it went so fast. I do remember being told that my bile duct had collapsed. The next step was to set up an appointment with Dr. Shultz, who is a surgeon. After questions and probing he was referring me to Dr. Johnson who did a scope of my upper GI. They thought they would do the procedure in Hays, but Dr. Johnson thought it would be better if I traveled to Salina where their clinic is to have the procedure done, just in case of complications. Good foresight on his part. It is important to mention that no one, with the exception of the first ER doctor, had said this was pancreatic cancer. I get it. With all the medical lawsuits no one wanted to commit. I did later get to thank the original ER doctor for his candor and honesty. Also I might add I got to thank Dr. Shultz later (he performed Steven's gallbladder surgery a few years later) for not being quick to operate which would have slowed down the process too.

We had not been sharing the possibility of pancreatic

cancer with anyone. I did have a private conversation with my boss, because it was only fair to him to be prepared as we were coming up on our busy season at work. Another reason for not sharing with the family at this time is as before I mentioned I am the youngest of my family and even though I was in my fifties, they still all treat me as if I am still their younger sister (I know I am and always will be). Also Brina and Lance had lost their former boss, Bill, to pancreatic cancer only a one month earlier, and he was a friend more than a boss. I did not want anyone to worry or cry or whatever.

A day trip on Friday to Salina was scheduled for the scope. Mind you, all of this is happening within the same week. We arrived at the Salina hospital and they prepped me for the scope. They were to install a stent to open up my bile duct and then take samples for testing. Well several hours later they finally got the stent in, but it was very rough and they thought I had had enough for one day (I felt like a freight train hit me). They decided to let me rest for the weekend and do the sampling on Monday morning. Monday morning they did the second scope. When they do these scopes they have a pathologist in the room to test the sample right there. *It came back as cancer.* That was the one thing we once again did not want to hear. We were asked what oncologist we would like to be referred to. We asked for Dr. Fields; she was Matt's oncologist.

I am going to give you a perspective from Matt. Although what I just shared with you is what I felt had occurred, he had a different side view of the happenings. You have to remember I was given a lot of drugs and I am one of those people who gets knocked out by a couple of aspirin.

Here is Matts' remembrance of that weekend...

My memory tells me that Dr. Johnson had the pathologist present in the room from the beginning. Dr. Johnson was to first retrieve samples from the tumors and the pathologist would confirm whether they were viable or if he would need additional samples. Dr. Johnson would then attempt to place the stent. Following several hours of attempt and failure they removed her to recovery while they waited for the radiologist.

Upon his arrival they relocated her to radiology where they inserted a wire through her side into her liver and through her bile duct. Following this Dr. Johnson inserted the endoscope back through her upper GI and using the wire and the endoscope. Dr. Johnson and the radiologist were able to maneuver the stent through the collapsed bile duct. This was all done in one long day. During this time frame I was escorted from the main waiting area to a private waiting area were Dr. Johnson informed me of his attempts and failures to place the stent; he also informed me of the preliminary diagnosis that it was pancreatic cancer and a confirmed report would be sent to Hays Medical Center. While waiting for the radiologist, I was allowed to sit with Jacque in the recovery area but they had given her a lot of meds and she was pretty beat up. Once the radiologist got there I was escorted back to the private waiting area. After the procedure we moved her up to a patient room and got her settled in. Like I said they beat her up pretty good and put her on pain meds so she could sleep. We were not prepared for this and weren't expecting an overnight stay so once the nurses assured me she was out of any danger I contacted the kids to meet me over at Steven and Danielle's and headed home to tell them the news, shower, two hours sleep, a change of clothes and back on the road to be there when she woke up. Later on Saturday after Jacque recovered, Dr. Johnson came and visited us and confirmed his findings even though he didn't have the completed report. We request Dr. Fields be her oncologist. Dr. Johnson would set this up and the report would be sent to her. My reckoning is that this all took place within three days. I did not stay in Salina but drove home each night and brought her home on Sunday. A side note to this was Salina was rocked with flu at the time of our visit and we had to place Jacque in the older part of the hospital in the pediatric ward where they were putting the overflow of patients.

So we traveled back to Hays with an appointment to see Dr. Fields. She informed us it was, indeed, pancreatic cancer. *When asked how advanced, we were told I had maybe three to six months if we did nothing.* She told us she would like us to see a specialist in the field. We had a choice between Kansas City, Denver or the Mayo clinic. We chose Dr. Kortz in Denver. A fun side bar to this is there are two Dr. Kortz in Denver, brothers, but in different fields of medicine. We were scheduled with the wrong one at first and by the time we reached Denver we were scheduled with the correct doctor. The oncology nurse set it up with our insurance company so that we would be covered for an out-of-state doctor.

The appointment was scheduled and we made the trip to Denver with scans in hand to visit with Dr. Kortz. The main reason for going to Dr. Kortz was that if anyone could operate and remove the tumors, he could. When we visited with Dr. Kortz he had a program that pulled up the scans and showed us how the tumors were affecting me. The one in the tail was no big deal; it could have been removed. But the one in the head was the one that had collapsed my bile duct was also taking over my portal vein. For those of you like me who didn't like biology, it's a big deal. On the computer he was able to slice the tumor and show us just what was happening. Later on I would remember those images over and over again to remind me, yes I had cancer. There was no way to operate. Dr. Kortz then communicated with Dr. Fields about suggested treatments. It was a disappointment to hear we could not have surgery, but God had taken over our worries by now and it did not seem to matter at this point. I was more concerned about keeping a "happy face" on for all those who cared for me. *I was at ease with God by my side, so I wanted others to feel that same comfort.*

Back to Hays we went (a big thanks to my Aunt Darlene and Uncle Ron who lived in Denver for hosting us that weekend, and also to my mom, who would make the trip with us to Denver).

3 – THE HARD FACTS ABOUT PANCREATIC CANCER

He said to them, "Because of your little faith. For Truly, I say to you, if you have the faith of a mustard seed, you will say to this mountain, 'Move from here to there,' and it will move, and nothing will be impossible to you." – RSV Bible Matthew 18:20
(Note: When I spoke from the pulpit years ago I used this verse. I related in my sermon how in this day and age cancer would be considered a mountain. Little did I know my faith would be called upon to move my own cancer mountain.)

To back track a little, before we left Dr. Fields office her head nurse asked me if I would like a pamphlet about pancreatic cancer; I said no thanks, I would just as soon not know. And I really didn't. Matt would research it online, but would keep to himself what he read. *I guess I just didn't want to waste the little time I had left doing research on the thing that was killing me. There were so many more important things to do. No, I didn't make a bucket list, for the most important things to me I already had... a loving God, a loving husband, loving children, a granddaughter here already and two unborn grandchildren on the way, a supportive and loving family and friends, a great job and coworkers, and a great church family. I knew I was blessed, but writing this brings home to me I have no regrets and many praises. So with that being said, let the following excerpts from the American Cancer Society give you a better picture of what I was facing.*

PANCREATIC CANCER FACTS

An estimated 48,960 Americans will be diagnosed with pancreatic cancer in the U.S., and over 40,560 will die from the disease.

Pancreatic cancer is one of the few cancers for which survival has not improved substantially over nearly 40 years. – *My maternal Grandmother died of it in 1985 – I remember thinking when they told me that surely after 23 years they should have made some progress in this area.*

Pancreatic cancer is the 4th leading cause of cancer-related death in the United States.

Pancreatic cancer has the highest mortality rate of all major cancers. Ninety-four percent of pancreatic cancer patients will die within five years of diagnosis – only seven percent will survive more than five years. Seventy-four percent of patients die within the first year of diagnosis. *–I had my eighth year in March of 2016!*

The average life expectancy after diagnosis with metastatic disease is just three to six months.

Few risk factors for developing pancreatic cancer are defined. Family history of the disease, smoking, age, and diabetes are risk factors.

Pancreatic cancer may cause only vague symptoms that could indicate many different conditions within the abdomen or gastrointestinal tract. Symptoms include pain (usually abdominal or back pain), weight loss, jaundice (yellowing of the skin and eyes), loss of appetite, nausea, changes in stool, and diabetes. – *I was very yellow and was losing weight; my appetite actually was bigger because (not to be too graphic) my food didn't stay in me that long.*

Treatment options for pancreatic cancer are limited. Surgical removal of the tumor is possible in less than

20% of patients diagnosed with pancreatic cancer. Chemotherapy or chemotherapy together with radiation is typically offered to patients whose tumors cannot be removed surgically. – *As you will read in the last chapter and read in Matt's e-mail below, mine was inoperable.*

Pancreatic cancer is a leading cause of cancer death largely because there are no detection tools to diagnose the disease in its early stages when surgical removal of the tumor is still possible. – *If the tumor had not compressed my bile duct, we may not have known. Again God was holding my hand and telling me it was time to find out what was happening on the inside of my body. You know He has to thump each of us in the head once in a while to get us to wake up and see His hand at work.*

The National Cancer Institute (NCI) spent an estimated $105.3 million on pancreatic cancer research in 2012. This represented a mere 1.8% of the NCI's approximate $5.8 billion cancer research budget for that year. – *Since I personally had pancreatic cancer, reading this statistic after the fact gave me some mixed feelings. This is the same as when I hear people talk about how great HMO's are in other countries; I would not have been treated if I belonged to an HMO. You don't treat lost causes, which having stage IV pancreatic cancer is considered to be, as you will see later in this article from the American Cancer Society.*

Please don't take this the wrong way, but on days I would have to lay around and just listen to the television, I would get kind of tired of all the attention (commercials) given to breast cancer and prostate cancer. I would think, "What about my cancer? What are you doing for those of us who have pancreatic cancer?" I have several friends and relatives who have survived one or the other, so this was just my frustration. I am more than pleased with the strides they have made in cures or treatments for any kind of cancer. Once I told Matt when he was upset with someone for comparing what they were going through with their cancer as to what I went through, that cancer is cancer and it is never what anyone wants or should have to go through, and if it is happening to you then it is emotional no matter the degree or type of cancer.

American Cancer Society: Cancer Facts & Figures 2014 and NCI Annual Plan & Budget Proposal for Fiscal Year 2012

Pancreatic CA Staging for pancreatic cancer

The stage of a cancer is a standard way for doctors to sum up how far the cancer has spread. This is very important because your treatment and outlook depend on the stage of your cancer. The tests described in the section "How is pancreatic cancer found?" are used to decide the stage of the cancer.

The most common staging system for pancreatic cancer is the AJCC staging system, also known as the TNM system. It uses 3 key pieces of information:

T describes the size of the main tumor and if it has grown into nearby structures

N describes spread to nearby lymph nodes

M tells whether the cancer has spread (metastasized) to other parts of the body

The T, N, and M categories are combined to get an overall stage, using 0 and the Roman numerals I through IV (1-4). The lower the number, the less the cancer has spread. A higher number, such as stage IV (4), means a more advanced cancer.

If you have pancreatic cancer, ask your doctor to explain its stage in a way that you understand. This can help you take a more active role in making informed decisions about your treatment.

Although not part of the AJCC staging system, some other factors are also important. The grade of the cancer (whether the cells look more or less normal under the microscope) is sometimes listed on a scale from G1 to G3 (or G4), with G1 cancers looking the most like normal cells and having the best outlook.

If you have surgery, the extent of the resection — whether or not the entire tumor is removed — is also important with regard to outlook. This is sometimes listed on a scale from R0 (where all of tumor that can be seen has been removed) to R2 (where some tumor could not be removed).

Resectable versus unresectable pancreatic cancer

The AJCC staging system provides a detailed

summary of how far the cancer has spread. But for treatment purposes, doctors often use a simpler staging system, which divides cancers into groups based on whether or not it is likely they can be removed (resected) by surgery. These groups are listed below:

Resectable: The cancer is only (or mostly) in the pancreas and the doctors think all of it can be removed.

Borderline resectable: The cancer has just reached nearby blood vessels, but the doctors feel it might still be removed completely with surgery.

Locally advanced (unresectable): The cancer has not spread to distant organs, but the doctor still can't remove all of the cancer. Surgery would be done only to relieve symptoms or other problems.

Metastatic: The cancer has spread to distant organs. Surgery would be done only to relieve symptoms or other problems.

Some people with cancer may want to know the survival rates for their type of cancer. Others may not find the numbers helpful, or may even not want to know them. Whether or not you want to read about survival rates is up to you.

The 5-year survival rate refers to the percentage of patients who live at least 5 years after their cancer was found. Also, people with pancreatic cancer can die of other things. These rates, called observed survival rates, don't take that into account.

In order to get 5-year survival rates, doctors have to look at people who were treated at least 5 years ago. Improvements in treatment since then may result in a better outlook for people now being found with cancer of the pancreas.

Stage:	**5-year observed survival:**
Stage IA	14%
Stage IB	12%
Stage IIA	7%
Stage IIB	5%
Stage III	3%
Bold Stage IV	1% - *This is me!*

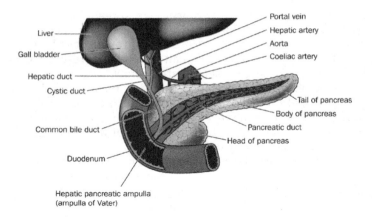

These numbers provide an overall picture, but keep in mind that every person's situation is unique and the statistics can't predict exactly what will happen in your case. Talk with your cancer care team if you have questions about your own chances of a cure, or how long you might survive your cancer. They know your situation best.

Last Medical Review: 08/01/2014   Last Revised: 01/09/2015

I might add here that it was very helpful to always have a second person with you at appointments and be sure to take notes or have questions written down to help you remember if you need to. As you read earlier Matt and I saw and reacted differently to pretty much the same information.

4 – MATT'S FIRST E-MAIL TO THE FAMILY

"Walking with a friend in the dark is better than walking alone in the light." – Helen Keller
(Note: God gave me Matt to always been my friend to walk with in the dark.)

We found at the beginning that we had a lot of people who wanted answers. Matt dealt with it by doing e-mail updates sent to a core of family and friends. Later we would find out that they were forwarded on to other family members, friends, friends of friends, some of whom we have never met.

Side bar from Matt: *The letter campaign started in conjunction with our trip to Salina. There were actually two previous letters not recorded and therefore not included in this book. The first was just an e-mail note on Thursday to family and a few friends at church asking for prayers for our trip and the procedure. The second note and truthfully the first letter was again an e-mail note I wrote upon our return from Salina explaining the results of their findings and what Jacque went through. This letter, though not recorded, actually began the expansion of the prayer chain. There were comments sent to me asking me to include others that wished to share our* journey. There seemed to be a growing following throughout the whole journey and I honestly don't know the extent of all who read these letters. These letters where written during the time frame of events with the emotion, passion and faith present during each moment.

Dear family: Wanted to let you know we're back in Hays. It was a tough trip but one that had to be made. Jacque did well but it was clear that the strain was affecting her both mentally and physically. This was the last piece of information we needed, we now know where we stand. The meeting went well despite the overall diagnosis. Dr. Kortz started the meeting with introduction, review of Jacque's recent medical history, reports of the attending physicians we have seen up-to-date, and all of the scans and tests performed. He set up Jacque's scans on computer and showed us in detail where the mass is located and the parts of the pancreas that are being consumed by the cancer. We saw where the lymphoid in question is located and what threat it poses to her condition. With the aid of the computer he showed us why surgery was not an option at this time. Not only is the mass attached to the portal vain it surrounds it to the point that the portal vain disappears completely in portions of the scan.

In my opinion Dr. Kortz treated us not only with compassion and concern, but also with tremendous respect. He dealt with our questions in a manner that left you with no doubts of what were up against. We spent a great deal of time talking about Jacque's condition and her options for medical treatment. We also talked about our fears and concerns for our future. Even though we will be fighting an uphill battle, with today's treatments there is still hope that surgery can come back into play at a later date. Before the consultation we were stressed pretty tight; shaking in our boots would be an understatement. As things progressed I felt God's presence take over and watched Jacque's stresses literally drain away. As we closed, Jacque's main concern was for her children, Erin and the coming grandbabies. She did not want her treatments to have any adverse effects on them, which Dr. Kortz assured her neither her chemo nor radiation would harm them. As we left the office our heads held high, we were resolved to fight.

In Denver Jacque's Aunt and Uncle took us into their home

and cared for our needs. Her cousin Valarie and her family continued to pop up with plenty of hugs and added support. In fact I would say that the Denver family is one of the huggiest groups of people I know. Needless to say I tried to avoid the hugs as much as possible but in truth it wasn't so bad. I can't thank them enough for all they did for us, and even though it wasn't Hays for the last three days it sure felt like home.

We now move the fight back to Hays. We meet again with Dr. Fields on Tuesday. I will assume that at that meeting treatment schedules will be set. So that's all for now. Matt

Jacque would like to thank all of you for the cards e-mails, phone calls and prayers. It is awesome to think of all the churches and prayer groups that are supporting us. She would also like to thank this family of friends and relatives who not only support us now in this time of need but have been with us throughout our lives. Thank You

Matt mentioned all the churches and people praying for us. We would find out over the course of all this that it reached the Middle East (we had family military serving there), Canada and England (we had friends who had friends or pen pals living in those countries just to name a couple). And of course I don't think there were too many states in the United States that did not have some connection to us through family and friends. Reflecting back it made me think of the movie "It's A Wonderful Life" with Jimmy Stewart. I am still amazed at all the people God touched with this cancer of mine and His miracle.

5 – DIGRESSION NUMBER ONE

"A woman's mind is cleaner than a man's; she changes it more often." – Oliver Herford

I feel the need to digress here. If you haven't noticed this by now, I do it quite often. I digress because I think you should know a little more about me.

I love to read. I can read probably up to eight books a week. Mind you this is just in my spare time. When I was young I didn't have a lot of access to books. I remember reading the same Bobbsey Twin book over and over again. I prefer to read non-fiction, except for The Bible. A couple of years ago I reread my Agatha Christi books of which I have over 80, in about six months. I like to read others authors such as Johanna Lindsey, Jayne Ann Krantz, Mary Higgins Clark, and Dean Koontz, just to name a few.

My other great love after God, family and reading is that I am a huge Royals fan. I have been a fan since before 1985. I have lived with them in the cellars. For those of you who know nothing about baseball, yes my sisters I talking to you, that means they are at the bottom of their league with no hopes of winning. I have lived with them through the years that other pro teams used the Royals as a farm club. I am a true Royal blue!

I am such a "Forever Royals" fan I have taught my grandchildren when I give them a Dove's chocolate, to say "Go Royals!" One of the directors who has her office where I currently work (Hays Convention and Visitors Bureau), brought her young son to work. When he came to my desk I gave him a Dove's chocolate and said, can you say, "Go Royals?" He went back to his mom's office crying, only for me to find out he was a St. Louis Cardinals fan!

One of my dislikes is tattoos. And that is being mild. As the old saying goes "a butterfly on your back becomes a buzzard in the crack" as you age! The only positive thing I can say about tattoos is at the end of the dance at Brina and Lance's wedding I look up and there is Matt's preacher brother, Martin, and Brina's best friend since kindergarten, Gracie, comparing their tattoos.

I also have a very dry, arid even, wit. My jokes have been lovingly been given a name of "mama jokes." They try not to laugh, but sometimes they can't help themselves.

I might mention here too is that both Brina and Danielle were pregnant. Brina wass due in June and Danielle was due in September. I'll let you do the math. Not a pretty sum is it?!

You're probably wondering why I felt the need to share these facts about myself. You will find out later in the book, but they play a factor in this story...

6 – RADIATION...

"Into each life some rain must fall."
– Henry Wadsworth Longfellow

As Matt stated, back to Hays we went. I also saw Dr. Prasad who would be my radiology doctor. They were going to treat me fast and hard. I believe he is the first one who said to me that it is stage IV cancer.

Before I could start treatments I had a pic line installed in my arm. There was no time to let me heal from a surgery to install a port. Since this is all happening around the Easter season and I was very yellow from the jaundice, Lance was calling me a Peep. How endearing! After my pic line was installed I was to be called their Borg. I am a big Star Trek fan, even though I hated it when my brother made me watch it when it first came on television. As you will see when you have a big crisis in your life, you either laugh or cry. I won't say that we never cried, but we wanted to laugh as much as possible. Sometimes we did both at the same time.

Along with the installation of the pic line they also made a mold cast for my radiation treatments; they need you in the same position each time for the laser. I also got three TATTOOS. UGH! I had radiation every day

Monday through Friday unless my white counts were too low. Oh I might add that even though my tattoos are tiny blue dots that together would probably cover the head of a pin, I still hate them!

The radiation began. They put you in your mold and tell you to lay still and then zap you. I shouldn't really call it that, because you don't feel a thing, but it does make a certain noise when they hit the trigger (do you like all my medical jargon?). Now they were zapping me four times and I knew I only had three tattoos and as I am lying there, I am wondering what's with that. It was easily explained; they couldn't really focus on a tattoo on my back. This got to be a routine and several family members actually were let watch the zapping, that once again my sick humor set in. Wouldn't it be fun to shake when they zap me to look like I am being electrocuted? Needless to say I never tried it, I would be dead and even though I see the humor, I would not let someone live with the remorse that they had done something wrong, because they wouldn't know it was just a mama joke. Some jokes are better left unsaid or not done. I don't know if I ever shared this with anyone till now, but if I did it was a long time after the fact.

7 – SPIFFY INSPIRATION FROM MATT

"A life is not important except in the impact it has on other lives." – Jackie Robinson

(Note: I know Mr. Robinson was talking about his impact on baseball, but I found this to be true from all the feedback we had from our update e-mails. Who knew how many lives God would touch with my cancer and His healing, it was overwhelming the to learn of prayers we received.)

Thursday 4-10-08
Dear Family: Just finished up at the hospital. Ok here's what's going on; they installed a pic line in Jacque's right arm which is where they will take blood samples and inject the chemo. We met with the radiation oncologist and got her set up for treatments to start next week Tuesday or Wednesday. Chemo will start on Monday and the battle begins. I keep trying to come up with something spiffy or inspirational to share but at the moment nothing comes to mind. I never imagined how hard it would be to watch Jacque go through all of the test and prep work. I know that God is watching over her and she is handling things well. I'm beginning to understand what people mean when they tell you that it is easier to be the patient than the caregiver. Well I've been

*sitting here for some time and still nothing spiffy to share so I will ask that you continue to pray for Jacque as we begin the next stage. Thank you again for all your prayers and support.
Matt*

At this point, the installation of the pic line was no big deal for me, but we were careless with Matt. Matt was not allowed to come back to the room; he had to wait in the sitting room. They had given him a time frame of about a half hour I think. Well about an hour later the nurse and I return to the sitting room laughing at some joke or something. Needless to say, Matt was not too happy; I don't blame him. The actual installation didn't take that long, but you have to wait for a tech to do an x-ray to make sure the line is in the right position. And I just didn't think to have someone tell Matt when it went longer than expected. Time had lost all meaning for me. I was in such a cancer tornado of tests and doctors that time just didn't factor in. But then I was the one who was busy; Matt was the one sitting and waiting for answers.

Side bar from Matt: My view on the pic line... I was angry due to the delay and thoughtlessness of not keeping me informed. This is partly true but there was more to it. You have to understand my perspective. Up to the time of the pic line procedure I was involved in every aspect of her treatment. I was in every waiting room, in every exam and every consultation. I watch as she was stripped of her cloths, poked, prodded and stuck with needles, many times in rooms with numerous people. I listened to every word spoken and if I didn't understand I asked question after question. Even in our visit to Salina, Dr. Johnson's staff would come out every half hour or so to check on me and update me on the procedure. Time had become precious and this little girl (Matt's name for the RN doing the procedure) knowingly or not blew me off with little thought. We arrived at Hays Medical Center, checked in at the desk and were told to take a seat in the main waiting room and they would be with us shortly for the procedure. Needless to say like most things in the health care system it was not "shortly". When the attendant finally came out she introduced herself and said to follow her, which I proceeded to do. She informed me I was not allowed to come back and there was no waiting room next to the procedure room and I was to wait here. She also informed me that it should take approximately 30 minutes. This I didn't believe but accepted the situation as is. Sitting in the lobby just being brushed off by a little girl like a fly on yesterday's leftovers, I must admit I was not exactly happy. Thirty minutes went by and I was still content but starting to worry. Forty-five minutes went by and worry turned to concern. One hour went by and emotions were riding rampant. Just short of one hour and thirty minutes I hear giggling and laughing coming around the corner. As they approached I stood up and I could see by their expressions that they knew I was pissed and the laughing stopped. Arriving home I made sure Jacque was settled but still being pretty upset I ended up outside working in the yard. Jacque can only answer the next question; when I came back in she was on the phone with the little girl from the hospital. The question I have always had was, was she calling to check up on Jacque because of the anger she saw on me and was worried for her or was she truly just calling to see if Jacque was adjusting to pic line.

I had forgotten about this, but I think she actually stopped by the house with an informational brochure. She never asked anything, but I agree with Matt that she wanted to make sure he was not mad anymore and that I was okay. He was never mad at me; it was the medical staff that would have felt his wrath.

8 – FINE IS THE ANSWER

"Fear not, for I am with you, be not dismayed, for I am your God; I will strengthen you, I will help you, I will uphold you with my victorious right hand."
 – RSV Bible Isaiah 41:10

May 11, 2008
Hi Everyone: Jacque keeps reminding me that I haven't sent an update recently and you may wish to know how things have been going. Well I guess I would have to say mostly routine. We recently had our Church 125th anniversary along with Brina's baby shower. Lots of family and friends came up for the weekend which is always fun. Martin, Matt's brother who is a minister, gave the Sunday morning sermon and was the hit of the celebration. Jacque did surprisingly well with all the extra activity but by Monday evening exhaustion overcame her and we had to leave the banquet early so she could go to bed.

Jacque and I are doing fine; this is the answer I give to most people. The meaning of fine is her condition is no better or worse; we are getting by and nothing has changed to report. To some this is evasive but in reality it is the truth, if I had something more to share I would but for that moment things are fine. When dealing with the question of how Jacque is doing, I first have to determine who I am responding to. To most people that ask how she is doing it is only in passing, they wish you to know that they know she is ill and they are thinking of you and praying for the best; they are busy right now and a quick fine is all they need at this time and it gives them hope. To some that I call the tabloid junkies the answer of fine is all they will get. These are the ones that want information that is none of their business; they seek you out bombarding you with questions and kindness in an attempt to gain one more piece of information no one else has. This is normal and most of us do it at one time or another; many of these people I consider friends and I don't hold it against them but in return I recognize their desire and the answer they receive is fine. To some though the answer of fine is all they want; they need to know that you are doing well, but too much information becomes overwhelming and is hard for them to process. The fear that something similar could happen to them is scary, and the knowledge of treatments, side effects, sickness, doctor appointments, and overwhelming bills can be terrifying. To them I smile and with the ever-so-slight nod I tell them all is fine. I'm not avoiding your need to know, nor am I forgetting the importance of our relationship with each of you. It's just sometimes the answer truly is just fine.

There is one more reason that you may receive fine as a response and is the hardest to share. Sometimes when I respond with fine, at that particular time, that moment, it may be all I can emotionally share. To get into details with others is to acknowledge the strain of the everyday challenge of dealing with Jacque's illness... the weakness one feels when you can't fix everything where the tools of my trade and the skills I have acquired over the years just aren't enough to make things normal any more. When the fatigue of mind and body are on overload the answer of fine is all I have left. Ultimately I accept that all is in God's hands and I should not worry, but the heart still cries and the word fine is all that comes out.

For those who have been patient with my ramblings here is the update that I expect Jacque meant me to give. The treatments have been continuing and have taken a toll on Jacque. Fatigue and nausea have become her worst enemies. Nausea has become an everyday companion, she has meds to take for it but the effects of the meds wipe her out. Finding a happy medium can be difficult for her. Fatigue can hit anytime but mostly after her radiation treatments. She continues to work every day but the amount of time she puts in at work varies from day to day depending on how well she feels. She is scheduled for five radiation treatments a week with chemo on Fridays. In the past two weeks she has had to miss four radiation treatments on Thursday and Friday of each week due to low white cell counts. They have been giving her shots on Wednesday and Thursday to boost her white counts and by Friday her counts are back up to the point she can do chemo. As far as I can tell she is still scheduled for a total of 33 treatments of radiation so I am guessing that each treatment she misses will be added back on at a later date. She continues to fight and in my opinion is doing quite well. She is deeply affected by the amount of work she has missed and she feels like she is letting everyone down. Her boss and coworkers have been very supportive and are thrilled every time she shows up. We have had some good news in the financial aspect, prayers have been answered and so far we have been able to cover our medical bills to this point. The insurance company did pick up a majority of the non-network doctors expense so that was a big relief. Never underestimate the power of prayer.

Jacque is asked many times when is the best time to call and for those that have been on chemo will find this strange, but the best time to call her is Friday "chemo day" sometime around late afternoon and early evening. I figure it has something to do with the pre meds they give her. I'm not discouraging you from calling other days but it will be hit or miss on how she feels; she may not be able to focus and may not take your call, then you're just stuck with me. Well that's about all I have for now and again I thank you for your prayers and support. So I guess in response to the question how are we doing my answer would be fine. Matt

I think this is my favorite e-mail or at least in the top two. After having been the care giver and the care receiver that is about all you can handle sometimes. I still find myself giving that answer when people ask me to this day how I am doing.

9 – CHEMO...

"Living one day at a time, enjoying one moment at a time, accepting hardship as a pathway to peace... "
Serenity Prayer – Reinhold Niebuhr

Matt took a chemo named 5-Florouracil, 5-FU. His hair thinned a little and he had an issue with sensitivity to cold things. He could not have ice in his drinks and when he got something out of the fridge he had to use a paper towel or potholder. He still has some sensitivity to the cold. My chemo was called gemcitabine. I would call my treatments on Friday's as "I am getting my shot of Jim Beam today." In taking mine also my hair would thin, but not fall out.

Matt had several family members ask when the best time to call. We told them Fridays. Now this may seem odd to you, but they not only give you the chemo they also give you steroids and other things and you actually have a pretty good day. It would be little different story two days later.

Not to be too graphic I found out what true love is during my treatments. You see chemo and radiation, especially in the stomach area, makes you very sick to your stomach. And they hit me with the heaviest doses they thought I could handle. Luckily in the two years between Matt's and my different forms of cancer the nausea pills that helped the most had come down in cost. When Matt had them you could only get three at a time for about $90 a piece with the help of insurance. By the time I needed them they had a generic at a much more reasonable cost. Matt would take care of me, clean up every mess I made, laugh and reassure me it was no problem. It didn't lessen the embarrassment for me, but he was a true treasure to me.

As I mentioned earlier I was overweight when all this started. I used to joke and say I got fat just watching Matt eat. He can put away more food than anyone I know and not look like it. Well we learned during Matt's treatments no matter how much you didn't feel like eating you needed to eat, if only several small snacks a day. Also Matt continued to work at his job as much as he could, which was probably a lot if you asked his co-workers. I had no problem eating. It was like I couldn't get enough food. You have to understand when you have pancreatic cancer your food does not stay in the body for long periods of time. I continued to lose weight, even though I was probably eating two to three times more food than I ever ate in my life. I would also go through cravings, sometimes it was salty items and other times it would be sweets (I had to be careful with these as I was monitoring my blood sugar at the time). I also worked as much as I was able to at my job. I would have gone crazy at home and going to work was my only relief. I would get annoyed when the fatigue would set in and I would have to go home for the day. Lots of times it was co-workers saying, "Do you think you need to go home?" They didn't know what they were sentencing me to.

"I would like to stress here how great my COO, Chief Operating Officer, Steve, and the Stromgren Athletics owners, Mort and Ed, were to me during my illness. I could not have had more caring or understanding bosses/owners. My co-workers are to be commended too, for all the help, prayers and support they gave me.

FATIGUE is the most hated word in the English

language for me. The Oxford mini dictionary definition number one is tiredness. It is worse than that. You are not sleepy, but your body can't function. You can't sleep, but you can't get up and move around. You're just stuck laying somewhere staring into space. Daytime television is not my thing. For some reason chemo doesn't allow you to read books, maybe short magazine or online articles, but not much else. So here I am an avid reader and I can't do one of things I love the most. I also cross-stitch, but that was out also because you can't focus enough to get anything done. Despite the fatigue or maybe because of it, I tried to keep things as normal in my life as possible.

A few things didn't work that way. I could still drive, but if it was across town or more than a few blocks I would let someone else do the driving. My mom took me to most of my radiation treatments. I felt safe driving, but I did not want to risk harming someone. I didn't know if my reaction times would be normal, and we also have some of the worst drivers living in our city that I have even seen. Oh boy, another side bar! Several years ago we were in another city and the driver ahead of us was not driving too well. Sure enough, we get behind him and he has our county license plate; I rest my case!

Another thing I couldn't do by myself was go to the stores. As a matter of fact, I didn't even attempt it because when Matt was doing treatments I would say I am going to the store and he would say "I will come along." He would make it to the store and then have to sit on the "old-man" bench until I was done. Not to confuse you, most trips to the store fell on our weak days after treatments; that is why we were able to go to work when possible, but not make it in the stores.

Here is another example of our love and how we have survived almost 40 years of marriage. As I stated before, I was losing weight. I didn't care about my clothes bagging; who buys clothes when they know they are dying? But one thing that does not work while bagging is panties (say it like in the Victoria Secret commercials... Sorry my mama humor again!). So Matt would make a trip to the store. He said, "What size should I get?" I told him I didn't have a clue. So being the woodshop builder he is he goes out to the garage and gets a regular man's tape measure and measured my hips. Now I ask you, how many of you women would let your spouse take such a measurement and how many of you men would think like Matt and just do it? Well let's just say it worked and I didn't lose my panties every time I stood up anymore!

10 – THANKFUL UPDATE

"When I stand before God at the end of my life, I would hope that I would not have a single talent left, and I could say I used everything you gave me."
– Erma Bombeck

Dear Loved Ones,
May 27, 2008
I know my letter won't be as word savvy as Matt's, but I'm going to try and focus and give you all an update.
Matt had his two-year PET scan last Tuesday and the results... (drum roll please!) All clear and his blood work was good also; PRAISE the Lord. He now goes to testing every 6 months instead of every 3 months. Please keep him in your prayers for continued strength as he watches me through my cancer. It has been worse for him to see me suffer than it was doing his own treatments.
I got out of the hospital on Saturday afternoon, after several rounds of blood work and antibiotic bags. I did have an ultrasound; they were checking to see if my stent was holding up and it was. I still have not got my strength back and have not been able to go to work, but have had some phone conferences to help where I can. I am now checking my blood sugar 4 times a day and have pills to take once a day. I am trying to remember my dietary training to help with my

diet. Dr. Fields is going to start giving me neupergeon (it's the shot that keeps my white count up) on a regular weekly schedule, so maybe I can stay on track these last few treatments. I have completed 22 of 33 treatments. So I guess the prayer for me is to get my strength back, so I can take some of the burden off of Matt.

I am wearing out writing this, but I just have to share with you all what happened at the bank today. When we were done with our transaction the teller (who we had not had before) asked Matt if he was Mark or Martin's, Matt's twin brothers, SON! What a hoot! She was a classmate of theirs and no, we didn't ask her name as we were on our way to our doctors' appointments.

We love you all. Thanks to everyone who sent pictures this week (Shanna did your dog have any after affects from eating all those bubbles?). Charlyn, it was great seeing you this weekend and hopefully in 3 weeks the weather will be better when you are here.

Love, Jacque

11 – THE STORY CONTINUES

"Nearly all the best things that came to me in life have been unexpected, unplanned by me."
– Carl Sandberg

I feel a lot of guilt over my treatments. I basically had probably three or four months' worth, probably one of the shortest time frames for receiving treatments. Matt had about seven or eight months' worth. I know they hit me fast and hard, but still I feel guilty. Don't get me wrong, chemo and radiation changes things in your body like nothing else; it was not easy. Most people take a lot longer and many more treatments. I felt like not only did I survive one of the deadliest cancers, but I also had one of the shortest treatment plans.

I had a few stays in the hospital when my white count or something else would bottom out. I had to have a blood transfusion. Now something you should know about me is I do not like the sight of blood. I look away whenever they take mine. Now to have a blood transfusion you basically sit for two hours while it goes in. I have excellent peripheral vision, so no matter how hard I tried not to see the bag of blood, it just wasn't working. It was a pretty long two hours.

I am not sure what happened with this blood transfusion, but about 12 hours later Matt had to take me to the ER. My blood pressure was fine if I was lying down, but if I sat or stood up, it would bottom out. At this point it was toward the end of my treatments. A lot of nights I was too weak to make it upstairs to our bedroom, so I would sleep on the couch in the living room. At the time we had a cat and she pretty much sat or laid wherever I was. I woke up with extreme chills and an acute thirst. I couldn't get up. There was our cat staring at me and I said to her, "Go get Matt." My voice was too weak for him to hear (the family provided us with a baby monitor after this happened). She just kept staring at me. Matt did get up soon as it was time for him to get up for work. I had him throw another blanket on me, my teeth were chattering so badly I could barely talk. He also brought me some water. It didn't take long and I had to make a dash for the bathroom; the water didn't stay down. And once I got to the bathroom, I couldn't get up again. I told Matt he was going to have to call the ambulance. He tried to help me; he thought if he could just get me to the car... But with my blood pressure dropping, I just could not do it. So he called 911 and the ambulance came. We didn't know it beforehand, but my bathroom can hold five EMT's and me. That's a fact everyone should figure out!

This was toward the end of June and my sister from Florida was traveling home. She "played the cancer card" on her trip home. She usually flies into a city three hours away and rents a car for the rest of the trip. I really don't think she was going that fast, but she got stopped and told the officer my sister is dying from cancer and he let her go on with a warning!

Also Matt was with me in the hospital and needed to go to the house for a few things. He called me when he got to his pickup and said, "Brina's car is parked by his and are they up in the room?" He was thinking he had missed them on the way down. I had said not yet thinking it was pretty early for them to be up. Well they didn't show up in fifteen minutes (plenty of time for them to have done so) so I called my nurse and asked her to check with OB to see if they were there. AND THEY WERE! We became known as the mother with cancer in oncology with the daughter giving birth in the OB. So all day long my thoughts were with my daughter having her first child and I was lying useless in bed on another floor of the hospital, and at this point thinking not much time on this earth left. All went well for Brina, except they had to do a C-section (one thing she did not want). Both mother and child were healthy and well! Since they were not sure what caused my collapse, they would not let me into the OB ward. So my second granddaughter, Elizabeth, was viewed through the wire windows of the OB. Yes this is sad, but at least I got to see her and was able to hold her about 5 days later. *Still thoughts of not being around to watch her grow up would cloud my mind occasionally.*

By this time I had finished my treatments and was dealing with trying to recover from them. It was a slow road but it was doable. What will my next scans show, was the real question in my mind at the time.

12 – FREE AT LAST

"But the free gift is not like the trespass. For many died through one man's trespass, much more have the grace of God and the free gift in the grace of that one man Jesus Christ abounded for many."
– RSV Bible Romans 5:15

Jacque Update June 14, 2008
Free at last. Free at last. Thank God Almighty; free at last.
Dear Family, Jacque has completed her treatments for round one of her fight. This is a time for celebration for she has walked through a valley that few have experienced and fewer yet have survived. No more daily trips for radiation treatments, no more chemo, and her pic line was removed so she doesn't look like a Borg (alien from Star Trek). I know that Dr. King's words were not exactly meant for a condition like Jacque's but the essence of overcoming this mighty task, accomplishing what seems impossible truly is freedom. The battle was tough and as in all battles there is a cost to pay. This is not the same woman physically from four months ago. Forty-three pounds lighter, walking a little slower, and discolored to slight ting of yellow she has surely paid her dues. But throughout the fight the sprit God blessed her with stayed true. Only in the last weeks did she have to give ground to her physical weakness and stay home from work. Even then as

tears streaked her cheeks her thoughts were never about herself but for those she felt she was letting down. Her family at home, church and work have always meant more to her than her own needs and to have to give in to the physical need of rest was devastating. Surely as cancer is the essence of sin in this world, God's glory shines in the soldier that asks and receives his sprit to fight. This is an accomplishment that comes with no medals or certificates, no parades with banners flying just the tremendous feeling of God's blessing and the right to say I made it this far. Today we celebrate, tomorrow we rest and re-energize because soon round two will start. Glory be to God Almighty, amen.

Wordy, aren't I? But what does it all mean? What's next on the agenda? Well basically we are back in the wait-and-see mode. Wednesday the 18th she will have a CAT scan, Thursday the 19th will be blood work, and Monday the 23rd we set down with Dr. Fields and plan the next course of action. Any more information I could give you would be speculation at this time. Surgery or continued chemo will be determined on the effectiveness of this round of treatment. This scan could also show inconclusive change at this time and we would have to wait a few weeks and retest. In the meantime she hopes to get back to work as soon as possible along with rest and exercise to regain her muscle tone and strength.

Jacque and I would like to thank all of you for your cards and e-mails on our anniversary. We didn't do too much just watched the Royals lose which is sad (the Royals losing, not the anniversary). We would also like to thank Deloris (Jacque's Mom) for all her help transporting Jacque back and forth to her treatments. Well that's about all for now, I will let you all know what we find out after the doctor's appointment next week. Again thanks for all your prayers, Matt

The next email blast from Matt:
June 21, 2008
Hi Everyone: It's been quite a day, one of those good news, bad news kind of things. First Jacque has developed an infection and was admitted to the hospital Friday. So far we have it under control and hopefully she will be released sometime Monday. She is doing well, a little weak and sad

but overall she is handling things well. Mostly I would like to announce that Elizabeth Kathryn Gerstner has joined us today at 6lb 12 oz., 20 inches long . Mom and baby had a little trouble and ended up doing a C-section but all is well; praise God. Due to Jacque's infection, she was unable to go into the maternity ward but proud dad held Elizabeth up at the window and introduced her and her Grandma to each other. Hopefully Grandma and Granddaughter will be in each other's arms soon. As Jacque and I continue on this rollercoaster ride, God's light shines in the eyes of this new baby girl and for a moment peace comes to our world. God be with each and every one of you and please pray for the three hospital patients that they will all be home soon. Matt

13 - THE ONGOING BATTLE

"Therefore do not worry about tomorrow, for tomorrow will worry about its own things. Sufficient for today is its own trouble." – NIV bible Matthew 6:34

7-19-08
"Therefore do not worry about tomorrow, for tomorrow will worry about its own things. Sufficient for today is its own trouble." Matthew 6:34 (NIV)

Dear Family: Another trip completed, another doctor consulted and Jacques' battle continues. I cannot say that the trip was successful nor would I say it was a failure; it's just another part of the ongoing battle we face. Again our Denver family welcomed us with open arms and allowed us to share in their home and hospitality. That in itself, made the trip a success. Not to mention the fact that Jacque's Uncle Ron and I, with great humility and grace, won the overwhelming majority of the pinochle games. And for Jacque and me, time spent with family is the greatest vacation we could ask for.

As most of you know the latest scans have shown that the cancer has not diminished nor has it grown. The first round of treatments has at least slowed or temporarily stopped the growth of the tumor. Or as I like to say, we gave it a pretty good kick in the (use your imagination at this time). But a second spot in the tail of the pancreas that we were aware of but not concerned with at the time has recently been confirmed to be of the same type of cancer as the one in the head. After reviewing this information with Dr. Fields, she felt it was time to again consult with Dr. Kortz and discuss the next step or options for treatment. Dr. Kortz sat down with Jacque and me; we reviewed all the information from Dr. Fields, and Dr. Johnson, and he showed us on the computer the latest scans. Unfortunately the results have not changed; the complications in removing the tumor are the same "inoperable" plus now that we have confirmed that the second mass is also cancer, it adds to the difficulty. He was also concerned about Jacques color which varies in shades of yellow and fears that the liver is in distress, and she continues to lose weight even though her appetite has improved, which means her digestive system is not absorbing the nutrients from the food. Dr. Kortz and Dr. Fields will consult and most likely start her on some kind of medication and supplements in an effort to relieve these issues. Most likely the next round of treatments will be in about six weeks and most likely be chemo again. Radiation in any form is not an option at this time or anytime soon due to tissue memory and additional damage and danger to her surrounding organs. The bottom line I guess is that we are in a time of healing, time for Jacque to recuperate from the first round of treatment, time to get the liver and digestive system working again, and time to build up her strength.

Throughout this whole ordeal we have continually seen God's hand at work. The everyday trials at home and work, the care and treatment from the medical staff, even the finances have been manageable due to God's guidance. The love and support from family, friends, church and our jobs have been a great comfort and I thank God for each and every one of you. The above passage from Matthew 6:34 (NIV) has become particularly meaningful to Jacque and me. To us it means living for today, sharing this precious time we have been allowed with each other along with family and friends, for tomorrow is unknown to us all. For me, this battle has been a wakeup call, a reminder that what truly matters in this world are the relationships and bonds we develop not only *with those around us but also with God himself. In our Bible teachings we know that no item created on earth will we carry to heaven, but there is one item I believe we have on this earth that will stay with us even in eternity for it was a gift from God and that is Love. Recently Jacque asked me if I miss my mother who passed a few years back. Do I think of her? Does it make me sad that she is gone? My answer was yes and no. I acknowledge that she is no longer here on earth but she is still with me. It is no trick of the mind to remember her or to share with her or even talk with her because her love is a part of me. Just as the family and friends who have parted in my past as well as those that will part from me in my future; who I am, what I have become, and what I will be is a creation built from these relationships and I will carry them forever. This is the same with the relationship we build with God. Someday Jacque and I will be separated by death; it is inevitable and no one lives forever, but whether its tomorrow or fifty years from now, we will always be together through love. Thank you again for all your love and support; may Gods blessings be upon you and your families and may your relationships continue to grow through God's gift of Love. Matt*

14 – ALL EARTHLY POWERS EXHAUSTED

"Your smile will give you a positive countenance that will make people feel comfortable around you." Les Brown (Note: I felt like this so many times. I wanted to comfort the ones comforting me, because I did not anyone to suffer on my behalf.)

July 26, 2008
Dear Family,
It is with a heavy heart and deep regret that I write you this letter, not on my own behalf, but because I am too much of a coward to face each of you with the news.

As Matt wrote we saw Dr. Kortz last week in Denver. The tumor is still inoperable, just from different things Dr. Kortz was implying to us we felt that we were at a standstill with our options. After meeting with Dr. Fields on Thursday this week we point blank asked what further chemo treatments would do for me. They are to prolong life not cure at this point. The short version, my cancer is terminal, but we were not too surprised as my cancer was at stage IV when this all began. I am getting a four-week rest period and have started the pills that Matt mentioned in the last update. Then I will have a CAT scan and do 3-6 treatments of chemo, they will use the chemo that Matt had this time. No time frame has been asked or given. I am pretty much pain free all the time. I have been able to put in half days at work here lately, which is a blessing for me, because I have always loved my job and the challenge. Fatigue still sets in often and is very frustrating. **Since we have exhausted the earthly powers for curing, it is all in the hands of our Father in Heaven and I have complete faith in his decision.**

Matt shared a verse out of Mathew with you last time. We found it to be a message from God, as we both read the same verse on the same day and shared with each other our reading of it; this is not the norm for us.

Some have asked if we will try to get a second opinion. Our response is probably not as we have both felt God's presence leading us to each and every doctor that has been a part of my care team.

My thanks go to all of you who have been in prayer, sent e-mails and cards, and have taken time to visit or call. I am not always real strong and it is wearing on me, but it is worth seeing you and hearing from you. There is also a world of topics out there besides cancer and I enjoy talking about them a lot more.

As Matt bragged in his last e-mail, he and Uncle Ron did some serious winning at pinochle. Well I was able to play a couple of hands and never had better cards in all my life.

Do me one favor, if you will... Do not be sadden by this news. God has given me peace, a loving husband, a son and daughter who would make any parent proud to say, "Hey, those belong to me." My children have made great choices in their marriages and have blessed us with two beautiful granddaughters and one more grandchild due in September.

May God's blessing be as rich in your life as they have always been in ours.

Love, Jacque

15 – OUR CLOCK IS UNKNOWN

"But those who hope in the Lord will renew their strength. They will soar on wings like eagles; they will run and not grow weary, they will walk and not be faint.
– NIV Bible Isaiah 40:31
(Note: This was Martin, my brother-in-law's, verse that he fell upon after his battle with a thymus tumor.)

7-28-08
Dear Family,
By now each of you will have received and read Jacque's latest e-mail. I concur and support Jacque's understanding of the latest reports from the medical team we have been lead to. We have not laid down our arms and given up the fight nor have we given in to false hope. All we have acknowledged is that the medical field in all its advances still cannot stop the life cycle from running its course. Each of us, from the moment of conception, started a countdown of our time on earth. To some its only minutes, to others a hundred years, but to all of us our clock is unknown. We could travel the globe in search of a cure, try all the remedies suggested to us throughout this battle, but in the end that would most likely just add to the pain and discomfort that not only Jacque is going through but the rest of the family as well, which includes you. We continue to believe that God can take this cancer away and that is what we pray for. But in part my heart

has become torn and my prayers now include that she should not suffer continuing pain and deterioration of mind or body just so she could stay with me. We will not admit defeat in this battle; from the beginning we understood that this would be an uphill fight. We acknowledged that our chances were slim to none. But we also understood that in our hearts this would be a win-win situation; if we won the medical battle she would stay here with us, if not she would receive peace with God. Easy words to say and believe harder to share and live with when it is someone you love for the heart still cries. Jacque and I have been together for thirty-four years not only as wife and husband but mostly as best friends. We have grown up together, shared together, laugh and fought together, and loved together. She is my inspiration, my nurse, my lover, my biggest supporter and my friend and confidante and I pray that I am the same for her. We often joked; alone we're ok but together we make one hell of a person. I can't imagine life without her and frankly it scares me.

In the last e-mail I shared with you my beliefs and that our relationship with God, family and friends is the most important aspect of our lives. Our relationships are not only defined during the good times but mostly through life's struggles, for in the struggles is when we let down our pride and let others help. To try and work through the challenges of life as an individual is a lonely and dispiriting way to live and I thank God for each and every one of you that has shared your lives with us. So now I must ask a favor of each of you; one of Jacque's fears is that her grandbabies will not know her, or have a chance to bond with her. So I am creating a baby book for each of our kids to share with their children. I would like each of you to write a letter to Erin and Elizabeth and grandchild to be named later, sharing a moment or moments that defines your relationship with Jacque and who she is. Maybe a favorite picture of you and her if you are willing to give one or copy it. You can use snail mail or e-mail, your choice; if you use snail mail please make duplicates one for each book; if you use e-mail, photos and prints sometimes get scrambled and are hard to transfer so you will need to attach it in a format like MS Word. Cards and letters would be nice, but remember write legibly, which I know is a problem for most of you, and remember, children will be reading this.

Again thank you for all your Love and support and May God continue to bless your lives as he has ours. Matt

Resting and recovering...

8-21-08

Hi Everyone: Just a quick note to give you the doctor's report we received today. Jacque had blood work and a cat scan yesterday and we met with Dr. Fields today to go over the results. Simply put, the scan showed no distinct change and her blood work is much improved. So at this time we will hold off on chemo and allow her to recover more of her strength. We will do a pet scan, blood work, and doctor's visit in one month, and go from there. We feel that this is a great report and Jacque is thrilled not to go through chemo right now. She continues to improve each day and is working around four hours a day. Nausea and fatigue continue to wear on her most days and by the time I get home she is beginning to crash for the day, but overall I think she is doing wonderfully. Well that's all I have for now. Again, thank you for all your payers and support, and may God's blessing be upon you as much as he has blessed us. Matt

16 – FUNERAL PLANNING

"The reports of my death have been greatly exaggerated." – Mark Twain
(Note: I just couldn't miss putting in a mama-like joke in my famous quotes!)

You have to know my husband to understand this next question. He doesn't like to plan normal family things. Well that is not meant as it sounds, but he lets me handle the finances, planning dinners and so forth. He pitches in and helps, but he goes with the flow on such matters. So one evening, he asked, "Would you mind if we went to see Cookie (that's what our funeral director is called) and plan your funeral?" He did not want to make decisions about what to dress me in, what songs and who would sing them, pall bearers, type of casket, which scriptures, basically all the things that go into a funeral. I told him I had no problem doing that. Now you may think this is kind of morbid, but really it is quite easy and we had a few good laughs putting it together. We were also able to find out answers about cost and how to go about the whole thing in general. Cookie did show us a $20,000 gold coffin, so later we told my parents that was what we ordered and I was sure they would help Matt pay for it! Actually I didn't think it was as good looking as the one we did choose. Every once and awhile I run into Cookie around town and tell him plans are still on hold.

We were able to get finances in order to help pay the initial cost until Matt would receive funds from my life insurance. Also at this time I would show Matt where I kept the entire monthly bill-pay information (which ones to do online, which ones not to forget and what time of month; you know the drill if you are the family bill payer). All of this was pretty easy to do. Even though I didn't know how much time I had left with my family, I knew this had to be done so that nothing would fall through the cracks and make Matt's life more difficult. You see I am his wife and as it was his duty to take care of me; it was my duty to take care of him.

17 – THE WOW FACTOR

"For this reason I bow my knees before the Father."
RSV Bible Ephesians 3:14

Along comes August and I had a scan. Dr. Fields said there was no change, so I was to have another month of rest and regaining my strength. It didn't break my heart to be told this. No change is better than a change for the worse. At this point every moment with family and friends is worth gold. Don't forget that we were getting closer to our third grandchild being born.

Always treasure your time with each and every person in your life. We do not know tomorrow and should treat each day as the last we will get to share our love with each other. This is meant whether you have been diagnosed with a killing disease or not. Time is precious, so don't waste it being mad, sad, revengeful or well... you get my sermon!

I can't remember how often I was seeing Dr. Fields, but at one of my appointments I told her I was running a fever every day about the same time around five o'clock. I asked if this was something to worry about. She said when that happens it is sometimes called a dying-tumor fever. Dare we hope? Had we heard her right? Is this possible? All the odds on stage IV pancreatic cancer say "NO." Also during this period of time I was pretty fanciful in that a lot of times my stomach would seem to scream. And I would always think, "Yes, I hope it is you tumor and my body is kicking your butt!" You tend to have fancies over the small things you feel, I suppose it is all part of the hope process, but when my stomach would make that noise it truly sounded like someone or something was being hurt or destroyed.

It was probably just hunger pains; I could not seem to keep enough food going into my mouth. I was always hungry. I was eating more food than I had ever eaten in my life. But you tend to grab each bit of information and add a little bit of hope; there is not much else to focus on.

Our third granddaughter, Shelby, was born on September 15. She was healthy and happy!

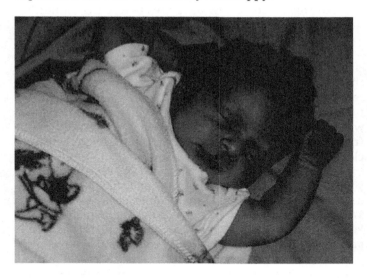

Time goes on and we were into September and I was to have another scan with a follow up appointment with Dr. Fields a week later. We went in for my appointment and were taken back to the room and wait. And wait. And wait. Soon a nurse pops her head into the room and said Dr. Fields wants to talk to the radiologist and will be right with us. Our first thought is, "This can't be good." **Pretty soon Dr. Fields enters the room and looks at us. She says, "The tumors are ninety-nine percent inactive."** I looked at her and said, "Does that mean they are dead?" She answered, "Yes." All I could say was praise the Lord. Looking back I think this moment was the most unreal for all three of us.

18 – SPREADING THE GOOD NEWS

"Therefore we do not lose heart. Though outwardly we are wasting away, yet inwardly we are being renewed day by day. – NIV II Corinthians 4:16-19

9-26-08
"Therefore do not worry about tomorrow, for tomorrow will worry about its own things. Sufficient for today is its own trouble." Matthew 6:34 (NIV)
Dear Family:
Seven months ago Jacque was diagnosed with pancreatic cancer. Six months ago Jacque started chemo and radiation. Two months ago word was given that earthly measures were exhausted all was in God's hands. Within the last two months we have planned a funeral, made financial arrangements for life without Jacque, seen the birth of Elizabeth and Shelby, and in a way started to say her goodbyes. Five hours ago we have received word that the cancer is dead. The latest test shows a 99% chance that Jacques tumors have ceased all activity. All Glory be to God, Amen.

As with any battle there is still work to be done. Even though the tumors appear to be dead we will seek further conformation through a few more tests in the coming weeks.

The stent in her bile duct will have to be replaced or repaired, and the question of what to do with the masses, to leave them or remove them will have to be decided. For now she will stay on her present medication for the liver treatment and enzyme imbalance. She still is weak and changes from various degrees of yellow and orange. Fatigue still gives her trouble everyday but the nausea has lessened. And through it all she continued to go to work. We had no sooner left the Cancer Center and she was heading back to work not only to share the news but too catch up on her paper work. You've just got to love her.

As always, we just want to thank all of you for your constant prayers and support. We both truly believe this is a gift from God and was made possible through your faith in Jesus Christ. Thank you all and will let you know what the next step is when we hear. Matt

19 – THE TUMOR IS DEAD

"I am determined to be cheerful and happy in whatever situation I may find myself. For I have learned that the greater part of our misery or unhappiness is not determined by our circumstances but by our disposition." – Martha Washington

Hi Everyone,
Well we made a trip to Salina to Dr. Johnson on Tuesday. I had a colonoscopy and an upper scope to replace my stent with a permanent one. Both procedures went well. They said I asked the doctor questions in-between, but I don't remember a thing. They did a couple of biopsies of the colon and the result came back okay.

When we saw Dr. Fields a week ago Friday, she let me decrease my liver pill dose to three times a day, but said I would probably have to take the enzyme pills for a long time yet. She also said I may be able to decrease them some as time goes on. I did have to have two units of blood a week ago Monday, as my red blood cell count was down. Not sure what caused that.

I still have weak days now and again, but those are getting less and I can feel my strength coming back most days. I do get frustrated when I do have a bad day and that just makes me mad/sad, but one day at-a-time.

The granddaughters are all doing well and their parents

are also. For those of you that have seen Jeff Dunham you would enjoy Erin's doing the routine of the Jeff and the Dunham. It is so cute! Elizabeth is rolling over now from her back to her front and Shelby is filling out and becoming more of her own person.

We are looking to help move Steven & Danielle out of their apartment and into a rental house over Thanksgiving weekend.

Well I just thought I would let everyone know the latest and thank you all once again for your prayers. To God goes the glory of my recovery, may He bless you all in any needs you may have.

Love, Jacque

Email from Matt:

Dear Family,
10/02/08
Well another trip to Salina, another test completed. As far as the procedure, everything went well and Jacque came through with flying colors. Just to clarify for some what exactly what this procedure was, it is call an endoscopic ultrasound where an articulated probe is inserted down the throat, through the stomach into the duodenum (part of the small intestine) and manipulated around to where they can see the pancreas, locate the masses, and insert the probes' biopsy needle into the tumors and extract samples for testing. While in there, they inspected the bile duct stent to confirm that it is still working properly. Does that clear things up or does it fall into the category of too much information? On the way home, Jacque wanted a Braum's Ice Cream. In Salina, the transmission locked up and we had to divert to Conklin Auto Dealers, who got things working again and allowed us an uneventful trip home. Unfortunately Jacque didn't get her ice cream. But in our opinion this was just another one of those God things; at least we were still in Salina we could have been on the interstate somewhere in nowhere land. As far as the test results, it will be sometime next week before any information comes our way.

In the meantime this past week has allowed time for reflection on this great gift God has allowed to happen in our lives. By now most of you have heard that at Jacque's last Dr.'s appointment the scans have shown that the tumors have ceased all activity; in a word they died. It didn't take long for this information to spread and the responses have been wonderful. I don't know how many people responded that this one gift ignited a fuse that spread to many others and caused an explosion that opened their eyes to God's works in their own lives. It truly has been an awesome experience.

But in turn I must confess I have formed some questions over the past week. No I am not questioning this gift. I truly believe that God responded to our prayers, as I always knew he could. I have been a part of this battle from the beginning; granted my role has been primarily support, but I have seen all the test and scans, looked into the doctors eyes when they explained their results, witnessed the deterioration of her body, and watched as her will and spirit were tested every day. I was there when Dr. Fields walked into the room with a look of amassment on her face and uttered words she never expected she would use in our presence "the scans show a 99 percent chance that all activity has ceased." Then Jacque's question, "Does that mean the tumors are dead?" And Dr. Fields response of, "Yes." There is absolutely no doubt in my mind of God's presence in that exam room on that day or His hand leading us throughout this whole ordeal. This is truly and unquestionably a Gift from God.

But as Jacque and I were sitting around re-living that day I asked her how would she feel if the scan was wrong? Dr. Fields cautioned us about getting overly excited. What if months down the road this starts all over again how will you respond towards God if this was only a temporary reprieve? For those of you who have had cancer, you may relate to these questions. Every time I'm due for another scan or blood work I can't help but wonder if is it my turn again. But how do we feel towards God when your world crashes. Each of us will have to answer that question someday but for Jacque her comment was that it could not shake her faith. For both Jacque and I, it came back to our Bible verse God lead us to "Therefore do not worry about tomorrow, for tomorrow will worry about its own things. Sufficient for today is its own trouble." Matthew 6:34 (NIV). For Jacque and I, sufficient for today is experiencing Gods love throughout our lives and this great gift *he granted us for today. Again I thank you for all your prayers and support and continue to pray that God Bless your lives as He has ours. Matt*

20 – LIVING WITH THE GOOD NEWS

"The quality, not the longevity, of one's life is what is important." Marin Luther King, Jr.

Dear Family: *10/7/08*
Ok everyone this is what you all have been waiting for; we have heard from Dr. Johnson's office today and the test results from Jacque's biopsy are in. We now have confirmation that the tumors have truly died. Test results show that there is no a-typical cells active in either tumor or her system. Truly all glory be to God; Amen. I would love to tell her story of recent events but instead I think it would be better if it came from her. Below is an excerpt of Jacque's response to a recent e-mail from my brother Martin (Dr. Rev. Martin Rolfs Massaglia) posted shortly after hearing from Dr. Johnson's office. I included Martins e-mail so you could follow the conversation. As for the next step, it is primarily is for her to continue to heal. There is still no answer to whether the tumors will be removed or how they will repair her bile duct; anything I would tell you now would only be speculation. Jacque or I will keep you informed as soon as we hear. There is still a long road ahead before Jacque will be back to any resemblance of the physical abilities she had before all this began. But it is amazing the changes that have already occurred. Thank you again for all your prayers and support

and may God's blessings be on you as He surely has blessed us.
Matt

Martin, one of Matt's older brothers, had a thymus tumor as a young adult. He would survive for twenty-nine years from his surgery, but would undergo radiation treatments over those years. In early 2014 those treatments finally take their toll and we would lose him.

Dearest Jacque and Matt,
Let me speak for myself and say that I appreciate the detailed explanation (definitely NOT too much information). Isn't it amazing that they have the ability to perform endoscopic ultrasound? So much less invasive than exploratory surgery... which they would probably be reluctant if not unwilling to perform. I'll be anxious to hear what the ultrasound reveals.

The questions that have come to you since the good news are questions I have also been wrestling with... And I came out at the same place as you. Love that verse. What better way is there to accept a gift from God without placing qualifications on our gratitude? I'm sure that you're wrestling with these questions so openly will be a big help to many people. Thanks for sharing.

It occurs to me that you may be having some other feelings as well. Having been "critically ill" and then moved "out of danger" more than once, I've been left with a kind of survivors "guilt". People had assumed that my illness would or at least could lead to death... When I didn't die, these very strange feelings emerged... "People will think I was faking!", "People will feel stupid for having me dead and buried". That kind of thing.

Maybe you haven't had any of those feelings. I'd be very happy if you didn't. But if you have, I'm writing to tell you that they are pretty understandable. And I wish I had just landed on your verse when I was struggling with the need for "validation" of what I was going through. "Do not worry about tomorrow" refers as easily to the uncertainties about what the illness will do next, the confusion about how to interpret this current blessing, or dealing with a movement from a terminal diagnosis, to a less certain one.

Hi Martin:
You hit the nail on the head. Not that I am sorry I am spared from this cancer, but when you've accepted that is what will happen, it is kind of hard to do a 360 about it, especially when you see this disbelief from your doctors, maybe not disbelief, but astounding surprise. I just got off the phone with Dr. Johnson's office and the report came back NO a-typical cells from my scope results. It is really dead. **I am with the doctors on this -- I have never heard of a stage IV being cured.**

I know there will be doubters as to how serious this cancer was, I have even had some, but then I remember seeing the reports, viewing the scans and seeing the look of compassion on my doctor's faces and in their words. Last time we saw Dr. Kortz he pretty much phrased our verse to us in "live for each moment." And then I wonder why God keeps blessing me so much, because I fall short of His glory so many times.

I am still healing and only work to noon each day, but I am not as yellow as often. Last night I even watched Elizabeth by myself, this is something I was not comfortable doing till now. I knew I could call someone and they could be over quickly, but still this was a big step for me. I am able to read books again, which is a real joy, but haven't tried to work on any cross-stitching yet.

Love, Jacque

21 – THE SAGA CONTINUES

"Don't watch the clock; do what it does. Keep going."
– Sam Leveson

November 24, 2008
Hi all,
Well it is another holiday and you know what that means for the Matt Massaglia family, somebody's in the hospital.
Details: I had my cat scan Monday midmorning, so after it I just came home and worked from home the rest of the morning. Well at 11:30 am, Matt comes home and says I better take him to the hospital. Again, this is a request I never take lightly because he rarely says it.
Anyway the symptoms were: tingling in his left arm, tightness in his chest and he couldn't focus. He didn't realize it, but he walked like he was drunk and that is not how Matt walks. He has had every test imaginable in the last two days and we are starting to get the results. Regular doctor says it is probably a combination of a couple of things, heart doctor is going to do a catheterization tomorrow, because his heart is a little enlarged; neurologist will do testing on nerves probably sometime in January. The heart doctor says we should have an answer tomorrow afternoon what we are looking at. Other options besides the nerves are maybe he had a TIA (mini stroke) or there may be some blockage in an artery in his neck

(one test read says yes the other test said no, so they will scope those tomorrow also). So I will try to update you again tomorrow.

Matt does not care for visits or phone calls as he is pretty worn out from the tests and they have been giving him big doses of nitro which gives him headaches, so it is hard for him to focus.

Hope you all have a great Thanksgiving, we are counting our blessings again as God is watching over us through this new trial.

Footnote: Matt was unable to get the results on his cat scan today due to the hospital visit, so will update you on that too when we know.

Love, Jacque

22 – PRAISE THE LORD – BEST CASE SCENARIO

"Accept the challenges so that you can feel the exhilaration of victory." – George S. Patton

November 26, 2008
Hi all,
Well, I was able to bring Matt home today. We got home around 1:00 pm. I would have written this earlier, but we ate lunch and we both crashed for about 4 hours. His catheterization went well and showed no blockage. They believe that it may just have been high blood pressure that caused his spell, but he will still see a neurologist on December 23 to check that he doesn't have a pinched nerve and cover the last of our bases, and they are not ruling out that he may have had a TIA, but TIA's won't show up in tests. Also he has a follow-up appointment on the 8th with his regular doctor, probably to check his dose of blood pressure medicine.

As far as his cancer CAT scan I was able to get his appointment rescheduled on the same day as mine, so we will have both our results for them next Tuesday.

He couldn't drive for a couple of days and no heavy lifting for a week or so. Thank goodness we were able to move Steve

and Danielle into their house last weekend, because Matt would not be able to help this weekend.

So we are praising the Lord that is seems to be as minor as just getting his blood pressure regulated. I am glad we don't have movie cameras in our house, you would think we are a couple of 80 year olds (no offense to those of you in your 80's) instead of the young kids that we are. In other words we are both snails in our movements.

I had to go pick up Matt's prescription today and pick up a few items we needed. This is only the second time in 8 months that I have gone to the store by myself. Baby steps! Baby steps! I am getting back more strength all the time and have not had to take as much nausea medicine lately.

We will spend Thanksgiving at mom and dad's tomorrow. But plans are to just take it easy this holiday weekend. Matt should be able to return to work on Monday, but is to only do light duty.

Well remember us tomorrow when you are giving thanks to God, for he has truly been blessing us a lot this year. I know that may sound odd to some of you, but 7 months ago we were unsure of my even being here for the holidays and Matt's case could have been a lot worse. Also our insurance has been a blessing and all the caregivers that God has guided us to have been excellent.

May God be watching over all of you who will be traveling this holiday and bless your trip.

Love to all, Jacque

23 – DARE TO BE UN – PC (POLITICALLY CORRECT)

"After a storm comes a calm." – Matthew Henry

Dear Family:
12/2/08
Jacque promised some of you that we would send an update after our visit with Dr. Fields today. She had intended to e-mail you herself but she wore out before she could write it so now you have to put up with me. I'll try and make it short, I know this is a busy time of year, lots to do, places to go, people to see and all that goes with the holiday season. Simply Jacque's scans continue to confirm that the cancer is non-active and in fact, the tumor that was located in the tail has all but disappeared and is being replaced by new cells. The main mass located in the head of the pancreas shows no activity or change in size and her blood work is returning to normal. In fact, Dr. Fields is allowing her to stop taking her liver pill for now due to how well her body is recovering. She still continues to wear out easily and fights with indigestion, but considering how deteriorated her condition was only a few months ago, she is doing great. She is now moved to the three-month scan and checkup, which, for those of you that

have had cancer treatments know, that this is a big milestone in your care.

My scans continue to show clear on the cancer and as far as my trip to the hospital last Monday for what appeared to be either a heart attack or stroke; nothing has truly been determined what happened. I got to spend three days and two nights at Hays Medical Center where they ran me through every test they could think of. I was poked, prodded, scanned, x-rayed, sonogram, stressed tested, and had a heart catheter to look at a suspected valve in my heart and my arteries in my neck. And so far, we have ruled out pretty much everything. All the doctors agreed that something happened but they're just not sure what. Most likely it was either a TIA "mini stroke" or my body reacting to extremely high blood pressure (I blew the top off the blood pressure machine almost). But they finally got tired of my happy personality, gave me meds for my blood pressure, made me promise to see my doctor in a couple weeks (which is scheduled for Dec. 8th) and sent me home. Personally I think they needed extra funds for the Christmas bonus but that is only my opinion.

Well now you are up to date and I'll let you go. On a personal note I'm asking people to DARE this year to be un PC (politically correct), stand up straight, look everyone in the eye and wish them a Merry Christmas for this truly has been a year of miracles. Again thank you for all your prayers and support, and may God continue to bless you and your family. Love Matt

24 – PETS AND CATS

"The best thing to hold onto in life is each other."
– Audrey Hepburn

June 4, 2009
Dear Family,
I know it has been awhile since we have sent you an update. That's a good thing. Matt had a CAT scan last week and I had a PET and CAT scan last week too. We also both had blood work. We both saw Dr. Fields on Tuesday (June 2) and received excellent reports. Matt is still showing an all clear except he has a couple non-blocking kidney stones, one in each kidney. No action to be taken at this time. His blood work was good also. My reports have again confirmed that the mass in the tail of my pancreas is gone and also the one in the head (the worse of the two) had a significant change (decrease). Dr. Fields smiled from ear to ear as she gave us the results. My blood work was okay except my bilirubin was up; we decided it was from the cold medicine I had to take the week before. My weight has pretty much stabilized and my hair has come back to its normal thickness (I had been losing it from damage to my liver during treatments).
    I still feel guilty at times for being so blessed by God and feeling so undeserving, when I see or hear about others who have not had as much success with their cancers. It is hard for me to believe that it is now close to a year since I was coming

up on the end of my treatments and was feeling so useless with having no strength, etcetera. I glory in the fact that I now get to hold Elizabeth as much as I can (which isn't easy since she is a solid little girl). Also I just marvel at knowing Shelby at all, since I truly believed I would not make it to her birth. Erin and I grow closer every time we are together; sometimes she wants her mom to go to work so she can come to grandma and papa's house. It can't be because papa is always picking up new toys and grandma always has a snack or two... All the girls are so different, and yet they have a lot of the family traits.

Steven is waiting to see if the GM crisis will affect his job, since that is one of their big buyers. Lance also made it through the cut backs at the college for at least this year. Matt is seeing the recession CHECK affect his work place as a lot of state agencies rented space in their building. Brina and I are very busy at Stromgren. Of course the summer is always our busy season and people still seem to be playing sports. Danielle still works part time at the school and they are letting her pick up as many extra hours as she wants.

Hope this finds all of you well. Love, Matt & Jacque

25 – ALL GLORY TO GOD
(*SERMON - JULY 26, 2009*)

"Opportunity is missed by most people because it is dressed in overalls and looks like work."
– Thomas A Edison

In July of 2009, Matt and I were asked by our Pastor, Rev. Jerry Sprock, to share our story. The following is that sermon.

To help you understand the "mama jokes", Jerry, our pastor, Bill and Kurt (church members) all like the dessert table at potlucks a bit much. Also noted by name is our Hispanic Minister at the time, Rafael, who was a very big faith movement for my full recovery on his own.

Note: Matt and I alternated speaking from our own personal journey. A lot of this sermon may be a repeat of what you have read so far in this book, but in writing the book and giving this sermon they are both based on the same story, so that is to be expected. There are a few new feelings and letting down of our walls, so maybe even repeating the telling of the story will, I hope, convey to you, the reader, of our faith and how wonderful our loving Father in Heaven is.

Jacque:

Let's pray.

Dear Heavenly Father, first we would like to thank you for this wonderful gift we are about to share with our church family. All glory goes to you for this miracle. Thank you for honoring our faith in you. May our words reaffirm others in their faith and will you guide and direct us as we speak today. We pray this in Jesus' name. Amen.

February 2008 I was not feeling well after a Valentine's dinner. I tried to get into my regular doctor, but was told that it had been too long since my last visit, so I was off his patient list. So in the next couple of weeks I tried to see if any other doctors had openings. I was having no luck with that either and about two weeks had gone by. I was more than sick by then. I could hardly eat; I lost 10 lbs. in a week (something I would normally cheer at, but knew this wasn't right) and felt my energy level just fading away.

So about the second week of March I called Matt from work and said I think you need to take me to the emergency room. While we were sitting in the waiting room the news was on and I heard for the first time that Patrick Swayze had been diagnosed with pancreatic cancer. And Bret Favre was crying about retiring from Green Bay. Matt told Brett to man up and we waited.

Finally it was our turn to see the doctor. The short story is: you have pancreatic cancer. That was the last thing I expected to hear that day. And no it wasn't really said to us like that, matter of fact it would be a lot of tests, doctors, scopes and scans before anyone would do anything but kind of hint at that. No one wanted to give us that kind of news without all the tests being in. And likewise we would not share this with our family either. But Matt and I knew and took the time to prepare ourselves, before we would tell everyone.

Matt:

When Jerry asked Jacque and me to give testimony on this past year I was reluctant and tried to bow out. To stand up in front of the church and speak about this past year is well outside my comfort zone. But finally, in my usual jovial manner, I agreed and went home to tell Jacque the great news.

Over the past weeks I tried several different approaches and thought I would do a top-ten list of my opinion of the best way to deal with terminal illness. But as this idea took shape *it would never quit come into focus. How arrogant of me to think I could give advice on such a subject. So in rejecting that course I instead will share with you a few memories of events that help me through Jacque's illness.*

Fortress of Solitude

During the early stages of Jacque's fight I found myself becoming overwhelmed by the magnitude of all I was being asked to endure. The roller coaster ride of work, hospitals, doctors, and even family and friends was leading to an emotional overload. The one person with whom I would share these feelings with was in a fight for her life and I was unwilling to add to her problems. As so often with God, he recognizes our needs and provided a solution. I had had all I could take; the need to get away from people for a few hours leads me to discover a place I called my fortress of solitude.

A state inspection was coming due on my boilers, which gave me the opportunity to hide in my boiler room at work. For the next three days, surrounded by the familiar sounds of pumps and motors, valves opening and closing, steam and water lines gently creaking, God gave me the opportunity to finally let go. For three days I scrubbed, painted, and readied the boiler for inspection and for three days I finally turned over everything to God. In that fortress of solitude I spoke to God, shared my anger and asked my questions, let go of my fears and exposed my weaknesses, and finally let the tears flow as he revealed to me that no matter what, no matter when, and no matter where, He is always with us; all we have to do is speak to Him and open our hearts to hear.

Jacque:

At this point I would like to stress that God did not give me cancer. God did not give me cancer! I say that because of the way I speak some may get the idea that God gave me cancer to witness. No the sin of the Earth gave me cancer and God used me as His (I hope) humble servant to use this deadly sin as a witness of His glory.

By the beginning of April we had confirmation that it was stage IV pancreatic cancer. Talk about really getting a low blow, not just cancer, but stage IV. I am not sure we shared that with too many people. We were focused on our medical team, tests, treatments that were to start, and so on.

Looking back, as I mentioned earlier, I couldn't get into

my regular doctor and Matt and I agreed that God was already at work and by our side leading us to where we needed to go next. Not to discredit my regular doctor, but tests, etc. probably wouldn't have happened as fast going through regular doctor's visits as they did going to the emergency room.

I started treatments about the third week of April. I would have radiation Monday through Friday and chemo on Friday. Pretty heavy treatments and sometimes I was unable to have them because my white count would drop so low it was dangerous. All I wanted was for them to be over, but at the same time it felt like I was wishing my life away. I felt a little angry with Matt in that when he had his cancer two years earlier, he made taking chemo seem fairly easy. I guess I have to give in and admit he is the stronger of the two of us.

I finished my treatments on June 14, about two weeks later than we would have if I had been able to stay on schedule.

At this point I would like to digress and say that at the very beginning God gave me an inner peace. And He also sent three people to tell me so. Two of them I have known for years and one of them I only met for a couple of hours. But they all gave me the same message from God: "You'll be okay." Of course I looked at that message two ways:

(1) God was going to take this cancer from me.

(2) God was going to take me from this earth to be with Him in Heaven.

That is the great thing about believing in Jesus Christ as your Lord and Savior. It's a win-win any way you look at it.

Matt:

Matthew 6:34 (NIV) "Therefore do not worry about tomorrow, for tomorrow will worry about its own things. Sufficient for today is its own trouble."

It is easy now to look back and reflect over the last year and point out the many God sightings we encountered. There is no doubt in my mind that God paved our way through this whole experience. From the first day we walked into the emergency room, it was obvious to Jacque and me that God was leading the way. From the medical care team to the family and friends who supported us, and a prayer chain that spanned this country and a few others, God placed us in the right place at the right time with the right people. So why worry? To answer that question would take far more time than I'm willing to stand up here, so I would just say because we're human.

I can tell you, this verse in Matthew has tremendous power; each day Jacque and I would tell ourselves all I have to do is focus on today; yesterday is over; tomorrow may not come but I'm here today and I going to live my life today. In this frame of mind the world does becomes a little easier. In a correspondence with my brother Martin; he expressed that when he was going through chemo he concluded that we can let the diseases of our bodies and mind control us, or we could go about our daily lives the best way we can, focused on the work God has set before us despite the inconvenience of our illnesses.

Jacque:

Mid-June I was back in the hospital being pumped full of antibiotics and so forth and missing the birth of our second granddaughter. Yes I know we were in the same hospital, but I wasn't allowed in to see her and it would be several days before I was allowed to hold her.

The end of July I saw my cancer specialist in Denver and was told no change. I didn't really get angry, but I thought of all those treatments and how awful I felt, so bad a couple of times I told God to make up His mind and either take me or cure me!!

Sometimes I forgot the lessons I learned from reading the Book of Job.

By this time Matt and I were leaning very heavy on the verse from Matthew 6:34 (RSV) "Therefore do not be anxious about tomorrow, for tomorrow will be anxious for itself. Let the day's own trouble be sufficient for the day." Needless to say I was a little bit awestruck when Dr. Kortz (our specialist in Denver) pretty much quoted that verse to us. He was concerned about the toll the treatments had taken on me and consulted with Dr. Fields (my Hays cancer doctor), and put me on some medicines to help heal my liver and make my pancreas work better.

My August scans still showed no change; so since there

was no change Dr. Fields asked me if I would like another month of rest from further treatments, treatments that were not to cure, but to prolong. That would have meant having another pic line put in for more energy-zapping treatments; yes -- of course I would like another month of rest. That's like asking Jerry, Bill or Kurt if they would like another brownie at a potluck!

Matt and I started talking about when we do we say, stop, no more treatments. We still had another granddaughter who was due in September, but at the same time I wasn't myself and not very useful under treatments.

It was hard enough making out living wills; there's still that thought of it's kind of like suicide if you tie the doctors' hands from helping you, but again when is enough enough?

The rest of August we would plan my funeral, teach Matt the household finances and get our ducks in a row, so to speak.

Matt:

Miracles

Jerry tells us that we pray for the miracles until God reveals otherwise. Rafael describes miracles as gifts from God wrapped up in the glory of heaven just waiting for us to reach out and grab them. Throughout the Bible we read of the many miracles performed by Jesus and others to reveal the power, the glory, and the love of God. There is no doubt that miracles happen every day and I believe that we were witnesses to one in Jacque.

But I would ask what the miracle was? Was it in the medical team? Which the combination of meds used on Jacque would lead to survival of others with pancreatic cancer?

Was it in the lives of those that were touched by Jacque's battle and through their prayers sought a new and stronger relationship with God? God's use of miracles touches all of us on many different levels and in many different ways; we will never know all that He accomplished with just this one miracle.

For whatever reason God chose to bestow this miracle on Jacque and me, it means that at least this day Jacque and I will continue our walk in life as we started 30 some years ago, together.

Jacque:

September comes and another set of scans. Well why not; I have already lived past the first 6 months. I get to be here for our third granddaughter to be born and am able to hold her right away. Of course everyone stands near by thinking I am so weak I will drop her, but that's okay too (not okay that I drop her, but okay that everyone is just being careful).

September 26: We are to get the results of my last PET scan. We meet with Dr. Fields today.

We are kept waiting.

The nurse pops her head in and says the doctor wants to check something; she'll be right here. Matt and I exchange a look and Matt says, "This can't be good."

Pretty soon Dr. Fields comes in the room.

She is not her usual self.

She says, "The scan shows there is 99% inactivity." I look at her and ask, "Does that mean the tumors are dead?" She responds, "Yes."

I say, "Praise the Lord".

As Matt would later write to the family, you could feel God's presence in the exam room that day.

Now here I would like to reflect that yes, God cured me.

Does that mean I didn't have to go through all those tests and treatments? No!

God lead us to each one of our care team. If nothing else but to show how sick I was and how great was the miracle He granted to us.

Would a lot of people that didn't have that confirmation believe the miracle otherwise? I don't know, but I think of the man who was blind from birth and how many people confirmed his blindness, and how that just proved how much it was Jesus that healed him and no one else.

Matt:

So if I was to be so bold as to give someone advice I would tell you:

1. Find you a Fortress of Solitude; share with God all that you are, all that troubles you, all that brings joy to your life; and listen with your heart for His response.

2. Pray for the Miracles; they are out there waiting for you. Through the power of prayer mountains can move and miracles happen.

And lastly,

3. Do not worry about tomorrow, for tomorrow will worry about its own things. Sufficient for today is its own trouble. Matthew 6:34 (NIV)

Jacque:

It is now a year after I was told all earthly powers had been exhausted. Needless to say my funeral has been put on hold.

Sometimes I feel guilt at having been chosen by God for this miracle when I have known so many others who have not been spared.

Did I cleave to this earth and lose my chance at a Heavenly reward? I don't think so.

Several times Matt and I have seen and heard over the last year how God has touched so many people with this cancer and the changes it has made in their lives.

And yet still sometimes I feel so unworthy to have been used as God's faithful servant.

I'm not always so humble you know.

But then I go back to our scripture in Matthew, or a favorite hymn, or hear someone else who needs a prayer, or someone who needs words of encouragement that our story allows us to help them because we have been through this.

Sometimes it seems so little to do for all that God has done for us, but then I remember God gave His son for us that we might live forever and He did it because He loves us.

As Matthew 3:17 (RSV) says, "For God sent the Son into the world, not to condemn the world, but that the world might be saved through him." Glory be to God!

26 – THE QUIET YEARS

"In times of joy, all of us wished we had a tail we could wag." – W.H. Auden

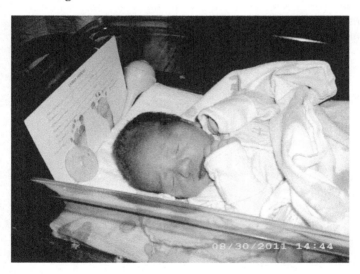

I am not recalling a lot that happened from 2009 – 2013, except we had the arrival of our first grandson, Jacksen, in August 2011. Steven had to have his gallbladder removed. It was otherwise pretty tame on the Western Front.

I know we still had regular bloodwork, CAT or PET scans, etc. Each time, there is the fear of some new cancer. It is a rocky road having cancer in your fifties. Along with aging you can never know if it is just getting older or if it might be cancer again. Once you have had cancer, it is always in the back of your mind.

I know that we finally made it to a Royals game; we had tried several times, but ended up having to give our tickets away because of one thing or another. I remember sitting there and Matt had gone to get something to eat or drink or both and tears came to my eyes. As I told you earlier in this book I am a true blue fan and I never thought I would see a game in person again, so I felt overwhelmed in the moment with so much emotion. I am not a person who cries easily. So it hits me pretty hard when I do. I guess I think of it as a weakness and a personal private moment and I don't want others to see me crying. We have made it to other games since then, but this one was the true awakening of the miracle we had been given. No I am not saying God granted me this miracle so I could go to a Royals game, but on the other hand, maybe He did.

27 – THE GOOD, THE BAD AND THE BEAUTIFUL

"You have to accept whatever comes and the only important thing is that you meet it with courage and with the best you have to give." – Eleanor Roosevelt

Now I am not a superstitious person, but if I could have skipped 2013, I would not have cried over it. Early in the year I injured my elbow at work. Most people will either get tennis elbow or golf elbow (one is inside the elbow and the other the outside of the elbow). Not me; I got them both at the same time on the same elbow. So, I had to go through rehab. They also ordered a MRI for me. I asked if they were sure I could have one because I have a titanium stent in my bile duct. I basically was told it would not be a problem. It is my own fault; I should have called my doctor myself, because later when I saw him and asked him about it, he told me I should not have had one. Would of, could of, and should of... I am not saying the MRI is what caused my next set of problems, but I am sure it did not help.

Then the following happened. I needed to have my stent replaced, but it is more difficult than it sounds. You just cannot take out the old one and put in a new one. What really happens is the new one is placed inside of the old one. So we made a trip to Salina to Dr. Johnson to have the new stent put in. Hours later it was not working. So Dr. Johnson set me up with Dr. Jafri in Kansas City who handles "difficult cases". This was in September. We were planning on attending a Royals game that weekend and also had a wedding on Saturday in the same area. Needless to say they scheduled my procedure for Friday (the day of the game we were to attend). They put me totally out (general anesthesia) for this replacement. When I woke up, well let's just say I wished I hadn't (not permanently, but maybe a week later). They really had to work me over to get the stent in place. Needless to say, we did not make the wedding either and headed back home.

  I know you are thinking, just a couple of things in 2013, but during this time I would have a round of shingles and develop new allergies or maybe flair up old ones. Whichever, I would go through a series of treatments and tests to find out that along with some known allergies, I would also find out I had become allergic to several of the products I handled at work. The itching would be so bad sometimes, that it would almost be painful. I am still dealing with this to this day. Do not ever make light of someones' allergies; they may seem a minor pain, but sometimes I think they are worse than having had cancer. I am not talking about allergies like caused from rag weed and such, but allergies caused from materials, antibiotics, things that you may come in contact with every day. People that do not have these kinds of allergies do not sympathize with people that do. I had a nurse once scold me when I told her I was allergic to the chlora scrub wipes and for her to please use an alcohol one. They believe you are just dealing with a rash that may cause you to itch, but if they ever had the feeling that you would peel off your own skin because that itch was so consuming they might understand more. Allergies are not something you can cure. I have doctors tell me all time that I am not a fun patient because I am allergic to so many antibiotics; it can be challenging for them sometimes.

Just so you won't think 2013 a total waste and to counter my self-pity, I want to end on a positive note that we had the joy of welcoming our fourth granddaughter, Hannah, into the family in March. Matt and I always try to find a special stuffed animal to give to the new grandchild. Well in late October before the due date, we found this elephant with huge blue eyes and purchased it at the time. Then March 22 rolls around and Danielle and Steven head to the hospital for the birth; I think it was before the due date. They left Erin and Shelby in my care. The girls and I had gone to a store or something and on the way home I was telling them about the stuffed animal. So, of course, when we got back to the house they wanted to see the elephant. We went upstairs and I grabbed the bag that I had not opened since we had bought it and the elephant had a hang tag with the birthdate like they do on a lot of toys now a days. Well to my surprise the date on the tag was March 22. I was not going to let Danielle out of the hospital without giving birth that day no matter what! Kind of mean of me, but she was a trooper and had that baby!

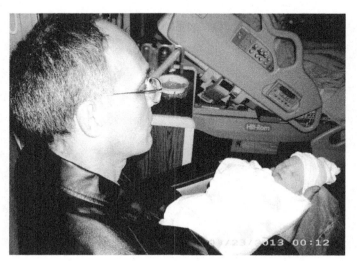

28 – GOOD-BYE 2013 – WELCOME 2014 – MAYBE!

"I have sometimes been wildly, despairingly, acutely miserable, racked with sorrow, but through it all I still know certainly that just to be alive is a grand thing."
– Agatha Christie

I can't recall what set the next procedure into motion, probably another visit to the ER, but we saw Dr. Johnson again and he then referred us to Dr. Osborne in Wichita. There I had a gastrojejunostomy. This is part of a procedure most people have who have trouble losing weight. My reason was not to lose more weight, but to help with my digestion. And it did help, but in June I was back in the ER. Now this was probably my favorite OF on all of my trips to the ER. I am not sure what my symptoms were at the time, but Matt and I both left work for him to take me to the ER. If I could remember this ER doctor's name, I would not even tell you then, you'll read below why. Don't get me wrong, the doctor was a good one and nice and was trying to understand my case and help me however he could. I really felt bad for causing him distress over my health. Finally, he set up a conference call with doctors Johnson, Fields, Rajewski and Osborne. And the winner was (drum roll)

... Osborne (they decided he could help me with this current problem).

First, after the short straw drawn by Osborne, we were told we were being transferred by "private vehicle" to Wichita, in other words we were to drive ourselves down to Wesley and check in. I don't know why, but this tickled my funny bone. It was probably my "mama humor" at work again.

Secondly, the ER doctor asked out of the blue if I had ever had neck surgery. My response was a stunned "no". But he told me I had a very nice neck for someone of my age. It must have been a God thing, because that small complement lifted my spirits a lot that visit.

Since we were transporting ourselves to Wesley, we didn't think about the time, but was a three-hour drive. Well we both had left things hanging at work, so when we left the ER we both went back to our respective jobs and briefed our bosses on what was happening, cleared up some items, then went home to pack and head to Wichita.

We finally arrived at Wesley around 9:00 pm or so and were greeted with "here is our missing patient". I think this must have been two or three hours over our expected arrival time than if we had left Hays straight from the ER.

Now the humor dies. I am to have an external tube placed (official name "stent placement using PTC" bilinary tube). I have never thought of myself as a vain person. I am not ugly, but I won't turn any heads either. Let's just say this procedure was my most traumatic. I now had an external pouch hanging out of my body to help drain off my bile. How was I to live like this? All I could do was cry. This was the biggest pity party I have thrown myself. What a sad person am I?

God showed mercy to me once again. I was to be released on Friday from the hospital. The head nurse came in to flush my tube, something she says never happens. Bile started to flow out my side, which isn't right. So back down to the surgery room again. The doctor who did the procedure was Dr. Brake. His original goal in placing the tubing was to insert it into the bile stent, but was unable to make it through all the obstruction, which is why I had the external pouch. When I came back to him for surgery, I am sure he wanted to cry, scream or something. All he could do was shake his head. I looked him in the eye and told him I had faith in him to do the job. I don't know if that helped or not, but this time he was able to make it into the stent. I still had a tube hanging out side of my body, but no pouch.

I found out at a later visit to Dr. Osborne that he had joked with Dr. Brake about sending him such an easy case (he called it a pud case), and he said Dr. Brake just mumbled under his breath. I enjoyed this humorous story.

Let me digress a little here and tell you that in March we found out our business was being out-sourced overseas and they would be closing our factory. A lot of stress coming our way again, I figured I would retire from Stromgrens and never have to look for a job again.

Well we are able to go home after they instructed Matt how to flush my tube and change my dressing every three days. We also found out that the tube would have to be changed every three months. And so it went, every three months we made the trip to Wichita to have my tube replaced. Then one time I didn't make it the three months. I started leaking around the tube and Matt had to put on the external bag. So with a phone call, they got me in to have it done early. Then I was scheduled for three months, once again. Yet again, it didn't last until the scheduled appointment. So I was scheduled for two and a half months. You guessed it; I didn't make it this time either. The next time they scheduled me for two months and I only made it a month and a half. I just cried and cried. How could I do this every month and a half? Also we would go to Steven's to celebrate Shelby's birthday, and I had the external bag on. I slept a lot while there, but Matt got to enjoy being with the kids and grandkids. Instead of going for the whole weekend, we just made it a Saturday day trip. That evening before we were to leave we were all having dinner together and I went to get up from the table and could not even push my chair away from the table to do so. I started crying again. How worthless was I? I don't know if I just felt a moment of defeat or if I was just overwhelmed by my own lack of strength, but it is very humbling to know what I needed to do and was unable to make it happen, especially with something as simple as getting up from the dinner table. So we made a call to my Wesley care team in Wichita and they got me in on Monday. By the way, that this is not a fun procedure. There is pain involved when removing the old tube and replacing it with the new tube. Again, we cannot thank our team of doctors and their staff enough for the great care they give to us. They put up with my moans and apologize for my pain.

This brings us up to November 2015.

29 – THIS IS NOT THE END...

"And know that I am with you always; yes to the end of times." – Jesus Christ

There have been a few updates since the original writing of this book. In July of 2016, we had to make an emergency visit to Wichita to install two new titanium bile ducts. Looking back, it was probably more life threatening than we realized at the time because my current bile duct was totally blocked. The most important update is, contrary to what we'd been told about no more grandkids, on October 31, Alexander Matthew was born!

Life does, indeed, go on...

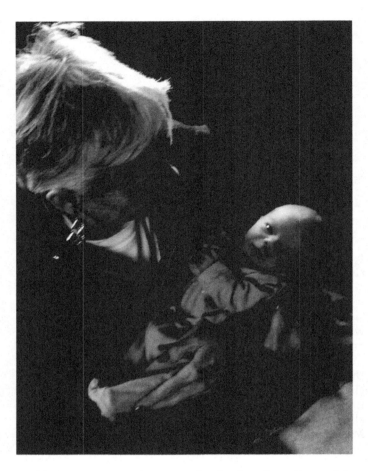

I have to say, trying to end a book, when the end is not really over, is going to be hard for me. I don't want to be one of those speakers who can't stop talking.

As I mentioned earlier I am a huge Royals fan. So you can about imagine what the 2014 and 2015 seasons have meant to me. Seeing Wade "wader" Davis hug Drew "hair-flipping" Butera brought back the memories of when Bret Saberhagen and George Brett hugged after the final win in the 1985 game. I said a lot of prayers during those nail-biting games!

There are a few things I miss. With the bilinary tube in my side, I can only take showers. One of my favorite things is to lay in a very hot tub of water until I wrinkled. I have the wrinkles, but they are not from laying in a hot tub of water! I no longer can swim, hot tub or golf (I wasn't very good, but loved to play) and am unable to lift heavy objects.

I do have a part-time job with the City of Hays in the Finance Department. They are very understanding of my medical needs and are to be commended.

Even though the increase to our number of grandchildren has supposedly stopped, we have had several nieces and nephews have babies this year or are about to have a baby soon. With each new life, I think, I am here; I get to be a part of this moment.

My sister, Charlyn, also had a very aggressive breast cancer and I got to watch her survive hers too. But we have had to say good-bye to Troy, Gerald and Myron, all dear friends, to name a few.

During the last few years, Matt and I have had the chance to talk with people who have been diagnosed with cancer. We have an edge in that we have both been the patient and the caregiver. It is amazing the doors God has open for us in this area. As I mentioned earlier I had lost my job, and I was able to take a temporary job at our Convention Center, Hays Convention and Visitors Bureau. One day a family came in and they were traveling from Disneyland to Disneyworld (you may know the story as it was on the news nationally), because their daughter with cancer loved Disney. What are the odds of my being in that place when they were coming through? They were amazed with my survival. Me too, and I am still living it! Matt has been approached by a lot of people with whom he is connected, to share our stories. But then we also have had it hit very close to home with us with several of our friends not being able to overcome their battles. And then my guilt will set in again. Why I was spared? I have had nursing staff ask if they can share my story. They don't want to break their confidentiality rules, and I always tell them yes. If I am to remain on this earth doing God's work, then I can't be selfish and not share this with others, even if it is in the third person.

Then there are a few uncomfortable moments. Earlier in the book I told of when Brina and Lance had a boss die of pancreatic cancer. When they would run into his wife, Ann, Brina said she always asked about me. This Fall at one of our local parades, I would finally meet his wife, quite by chance. She recognized Elizabeth with me as being Brina's daughter. Matt knew her, but I had never met her. She could not have been nicer to me. I could only express my sadness for her loss and hoped she was doing well. You see as Matt said earlier, one never forgets a loved one. She shed a few tears and I felt bad that I had brought back those sad memories for her. I know I am the only one feeling the guilt for my survival, but it doesn't lessen my feeling pain for those who have lost their loved ones.

If you took the time to look over the data on pancreatic cancer chapter, you can see that I am truly a miracle. I was given a 1% survival, maybe a five-year survival at the outside. In March 2016 I reached my eight-year anniversary from diagnosis. I don't know what is still to come, but I think I will stick with God's advice:

"Therefore do not worry about tomorrow, for tomorrow will worry about its own things. Sufficient for today is its own trouble." – Matthew 6:34 (NIV)

ABOUT THE AUTHOR

Jacque Massaglia penned this work of truth after experiencing true miracles in her life. Through her journey, she discovered that miracles can happen every day for everyone. Her dream is to share this story with others, hoping it can inspire them to see how a faith-based life can change their life as well. In addition to being a writer, Jacque is a loving wife, mother, grandmother, aunt and friend; she resides in Hays, Kansas.

Made in the USA
Las Vegas, NV
20 September 2023